UNDISCOVERED

UNDISCOVERED

The Fascinating World of
Undiscovered Places, Graves, Wrecks,
and Treasure

IAN WILSON

BTB
BEECH TREE BOOKS
WILLIAM MORROW
New York

1   S

Copyright © 1987 by Ian Wilson

First published in Great Britain by
Michael O'Mara Books Ltd

Library of Congress Catalog Card Number: 86-73044

ISBN: 0-688-07278-X

Printed in Great Britain
First U.S. Edition
1 2 3 4 5 6 7 8 9 10

Editors: Erica Hunningher and Fiona Holman
Design: Design 23
Picture research: Helena Beaufoy
Indexer: Valerie Chandler

*TITLE PAGE: The moment of discovery, 1922. The British
Egyptologist Howard Carter opens up the golden shrine
of the tomb of the pharoah Tutankhamun. What similar
discoveries could the future hold?*

BTB

The word "book" is said to derive from *boka*, or beech.
The beech tree has been the patron tree of writers since ancient times and
represents the flowering of literature and knowledge.

CONTENTS

Author's Preface   6
Introduction: The New World of Discovery   7
   opened up in Recent Years

PART I: Undiscovered Places   14
The Biblical Cities of Sodom and Gomorrah   16
The Lost Land of Atlantis   21
The Greek City of Helike   27
The Battlefield of Alesia   31
Pompeii's Lost Neighbours   36
The Battlefield of Mount Badon   41

PART II: Undiscovered Graves   46
Lost Tombs of the Ancient Egyptians   48
The Tomb of China's First Emperor   55
The Tomb of Antiochus of Commagene   60
The Tomb of Herod the Great   64
The Grave of Attila the Hun   69
The Grave of King Arthur   73
The Unburied King: James IV, King of Scots   80
Sir Francis Drake's Lead Coffin   86
Henry Hudson and his Companions   92
Everest Climbers, Mallory and Irvine   97

PART III: Undiscovered Wrecks   102
The Greek Statues Wreck   104
The Lost White Ship   108
The Ships of Columbus   112
Sir Richard Grenville's Revenge   120
Sir Francis Drake's Golden Hind   125
John Paul Jones's Bonhomme Richard   131

PART IV: Undiscovered Treasure   136
Treasures of Homer's Troy?   138
The Treasure of the Dead Sea Scrolls 144
King John's 'Jewels'   151
The Gold of El Dorado   158
The Basing House Hoard   165
Bonnie Prince Charlie's Army Payroll 171
The Gold of the Royal Charter   175
The Gold of Custer's Last Stand   181

A Chronology of the Discovered   186
Index   190

Author's Preface

The idea and title for *Undiscovered* were conceived as early as 1982, but perhaps because it would seem impossible to write a whole book about what has *not* been found, it took three years before, during a weekend stay at my home, the project was enthusiastically taken up by my publishers, Michael and Lesley O'Mara.

In fact, the world is full of so many unearthed ancient places, undiscovered graves, unlocated wrecks, missing paintings and lost treasures that the problem has been not so much what to put into the book as what to leave out. For reasons of space, for instance, an already written section devoted to undiscovered works of art has been omitted from this volume in anticipation of an *Undiscovered 2*.

Since the entries in this book are all ripe and live for rediscovery by anyone at any time, I have tried wherever possible to obtain the very latest information, and my grateful thanks are due to the many specialists who generously helped with this. These included Professor John McRay [Herod the Great]; Mr Sydney Wignall [Sir Francis Drake, *Revenge, Bonhomme Richard* and *Royal Charter*]; Mr Peter Marsden [*Golden Hind*]; Mr A. S. Irvine and Mr William Summers [Mallory and Irvine]; and Mr Dennis Jackson of the Hampshire County Council [The Basing House Treasure].

If finding pictures for *Undiscovered* might have seemed even more impossible than writing about it, picture researcher Helena Beaufoy managed this miracle while in the full bloom of imminent motherhood. My thanks are also due to editors, Erica Hunningher and Fiona Holman for their continual patience and attention to detail, Sarah Coombe for her enthusiastic overseeing of the project, and not least to Michael and Lesley O'Mara (also in imminent parenthood) for their generous and amiable support all the way.

IAN WILSON AUGUST 1986
BRISTOL ENGLAND

Introduction

THE NEW WORLD OF DISCOVERY
OPENED UP IN RECENT YEARS

With hundreds of millions of pounds today being spent on the exploration of space, it might be thought that on this planet there is little left to be discovered, that there is scarcely a corner we are not able to get to, or view from some 'spy' satellite.

Yet, there is one very real field in which the opportunity for discovery has never been greater: that of the lost world of the past, both the recent past, and that of many centuries ago. Within the recent months that this book has been in preparation for publication there have been released the second set of dramatic photographs of the ill-fated liner *Titanic*, sunk seventy-three years ago, and in 1985 relocated two miles down on the bed of the Atlantic. From Egypt has come news of the rediscovery at Saqqara in Egypt of the tomb of Maya, treasurer to the boy pharaoh Tutankhamun. From the wreck of a Dutch East Indiaman, the *Geldermalsen*, sunk in the South China Sea in 1752, have been retrieved the 150,000 pieces of magnificent Chinese porcelain known as the Nanking Cargo. Nor has it been very long since British

1985: amid the wreck of the Geldermalsen, *mint-condition Chinese porcelain awaits recovery after over 200 years beneath the South China Sea.*

television viewers thrilled to one of the country's most public of archaeological moments, the bringing to the surface from the waters of the Solent of Henry VIII's warship *Mary Rose*, lost, apparently beyond recovery, since her dramatic sinking before Henry VIII's gaze on 19 July 1545.

The fascination of such discoveries is not, or should not be, one of any mere lure of gold. The *Mary Rose* does appear to have yielded the occasional gold coin, but there would be few of those who worked on her who would claim that such finds were high on their list of expectations. As is quite evident from the accounts of some of their experiences, the greater attraction was the altogether more subtle one of coming face to face with the historical past, sometimes quite literally so, as in the case of one of Prince Charles's dives, by confronting, face to face, the skull of an unfortunate Tudor seaman trapped below decks as the ship went down. As has been remarked by Colin Renfrew, Disney Professor of Archaeology at the University of Cambridge: 'The really exciting discoveries are not the precious metals, but the ones that advance our knowledge of the human past, how we came to be where we are today. . . . The one thing we know for sure is that we don't know very much yet; there are plenty of surprises in store.'

1986: two miles down on the bed of the Atlantic the latest underwater exploration gadgetry illuminates a part of the ill-fated Titanic.

So why has there been such a plethora of new discoveries in recent years, ranging from the successful location and recovery of the gold bullion on board HMS *Edinburgh* to the finding of the tomb of the second century BC Han Dynasty Chinese emperor Wen Di? A fundamental reason has been the sheer wealth of new opportunities for discovery of the past opened up by new technology, particularly in terms of underwater exploration. Despite the great advances in scuba diving made since the Second World War, it may not yet be possible for men to move freely two miles down beneath the chill waters of the Atlantic. But a simple substitute for human presence can be robot submarines equipped with underwater lights and television cameras, and it was with precisely such aids that the American Woods Hole Oceanographic Institute managed to make their dramatic relocation of the *Titanic* during 1985, since followed up with explorations inside the ship itself.

Of course, not all wrecks are as large as the *Titanic*, and are correspondingly less likely to remain visible, particularly if they were made of wood, and foundered several centuries ago. In a river estuary shipwrecks may quickly become invisible beneath a covering of silt. In tropical waters they may become disguised by accretions of coral. But to the aid of just such problems has come the side-scanning sonar developed by Dr Harold Edgerton of the Massachusetts Institute of Technology. As early as July 1968 a survey by Edgerton of the likely *Mary Rose* site not only confirmed the presence of the ancient wreck, it even indicated that the ship was lying heeled over, with one side preserved, the other largely missing, exactly as subsequent excavation proved.

And as rapid as the rise in techniques for the location of lost artefacts has been the development of methods of preserving these, particularly in the light of the surprisingly good condition in which many items have been found after long centuries underwater. Due to the effective embalming properties of Solent silt the *Mary Rose* furnished leather footwear, purses and satchels, a formidable medical kit from the barber surgeon's cabin, musical instruments, an armoury of still supple longbows and arrows, carpenters' tools, some delicate navigational instruments, effectively a whole time-capsule of life as it had been on the *Mary Rose* up to the moment the ship went down. And as recent land archaeology has shown, even where an ancient burial appears to be completely rotted away, careful detection and treatment of soil discolorations can enable the reconstruction of that burial, even from as long ago as Anglo-Saxon times.

So, given the wealth of new technology available, the question that arises is what might still lie in wait to be discovered, if sufficient resources and energy could be directed to the search? It is this which is the purpose of this book, to offer a taste of the sort of 'lost' ancient places and items likely to be waiting somewhere, whether under the earth, or under some ocean sea-bed, for someone to bring them to the light of day. For those with a penchant for 'treasure' I have even provided suggestions of some of the less fanciful from the hundreds of tales of lost hoards, (many of these latter, including that of Rennes-le-Château, needing to be taken with more than a large pinch of salt).

But in the midst of whatever enthusiasm might be generated for the recovery of lost objects from the past, a word of caution is also required. As this author is very much aware, the exciting new possibilities for opening up the world of the past are not without their accompanying hazards, particularly if taken up by the wrong

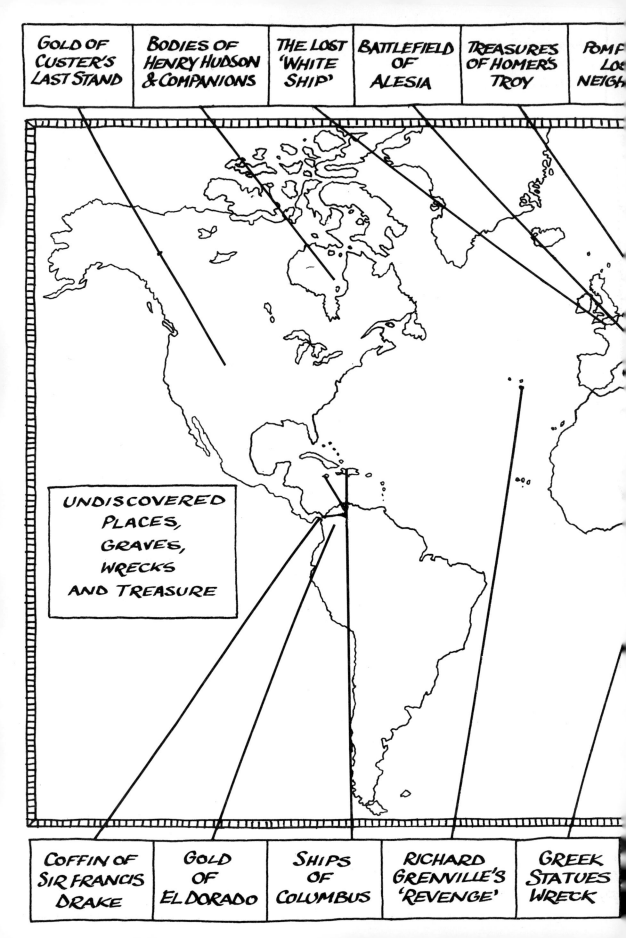

GOLD OF CUSTER'S LAST STAND

BODIES OF HENRY HUDSON & COMPANIONS

THE LOST 'WHITE SHIP'

BATTLEFIELD OF ALESIA

TREASURES OF HOMER'S TROY

POMP LOS NEIGH

UNDISCOVERED PLACES, GRAVES, WRECKS AND TREASURE

COFFIN OF SIR FRANCIS DRAKE

GOLD OF EL DORADO

SHIPS OF COLUMBUS

RICHARD GRENVILLE'S 'REVENGE'

GREEK STATUES WRECK

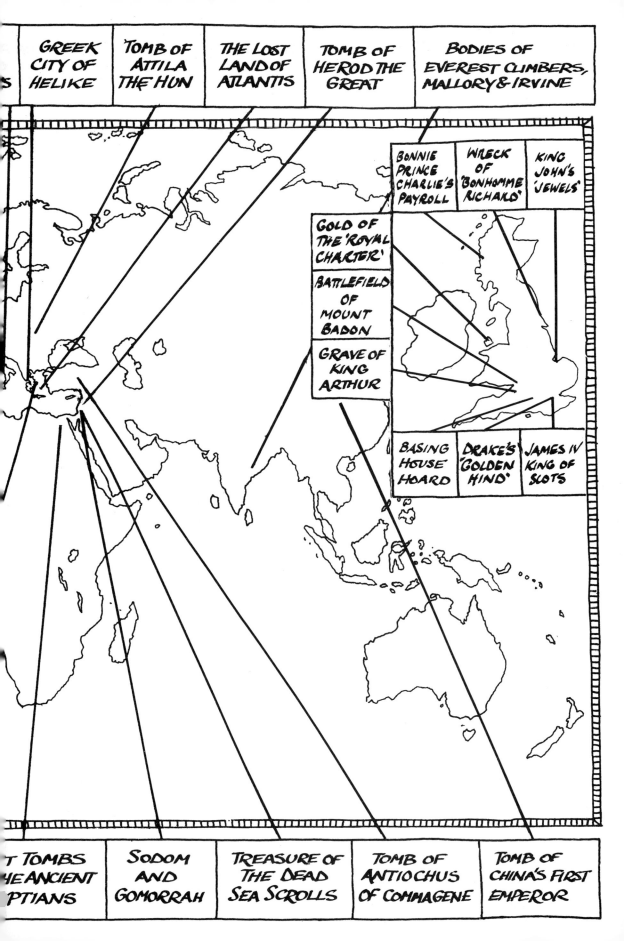

GREEK CITY OF HELIKE

TOMB OF ATTILA THE HUN

THE LOST LAND OF ATLANTIS

TOMB OF HEROD THE GREAT

BODIES OF EVEREST CLIMBERS, MALLORY & IRVINE

BONNIE PRINCE CHARLIE'S PAYROLL

WRECK OF 'BONHOMME RICHARD'

KING JOHN'S 'JEWELS'

GOLD OF THE 'ROYAL CHARTER'

BATTLEFIELD OF MOUNT BADON

GRAVE OF KING ARTHUR

BASING HOUSE HOARD

DRAKE'S 'GOLDEN HIND'

JAMES IV KING OF SCOTS

TOMBS HE ANCIENT PTIANS

SODOM AND GOMORRAH

TREASURE OF THE DEAD SEA SCROLLS

TOMB OF ANTIOCHUS OF COMMAGENE

TOMB OF CHINA'S FIRST EMPEROR

Recovered after more than 450 years, part of the hull of Henry VIII's warship Mary Rose *undergoing conservation at Portsmouth Naval Base*

hands. It so happens that some of the very same technological developments which have brought 'lost' historical items nearer to recovery have also made such projects easier for that individual most despised by modern-day archaeologists, the amateur 'treasure-hunter' or 'T.H.er' as he is called. As they sweep the ground with their metal-detectors, listening for the tell-tale signals that may denote the presence of some buried shoe-buckle or ancient coin, treasure-hunters frequently claim that they have a genuine interest in the past, and that the criticisms levelled against them by archaeologists are unfair. Treasure-hunter clubs and magazines reinforce the image of apparent respectability.

But the blunt truth is that while there is nothing wrong in looking for lost objects from the past, and nothing wrong in trying to find the occasional crock of gold at the end of the rainbow, such tasks are rarely ones that should be entrusted to the enthusiastic amateur, whether working alone or with a metal-detecting club. Precisely because so much can now be learned of the past, so it is only right that searches both on land and underwater should be carried out under the direction of professionals. Since, even in the most professional of projects there is almost invariably the need for amateur help, opportunities for which are usually advertised in archaeological magazines, there is no need for anyone to feel excluded by the 'academic prejudice' sometimes claimed.

Regrettably, there continue to be some instances of irresponsible behaviour by 'treasure-hunters', but both in Britain and overseas appropriate legislation (although not always strong enough) is gradually being brought in. The British law of 'treasure trove' which has been in force for many years, requires the surrender to the Crown of all discovered hoards of gold and silver, there usually being paid a generous compensation of a fair market value to those who abide by the rules. The Ancient Monuments and Archaeological Areas Act of 1979 lays down some protection against incursions into more obvious sites of archaeological interest. And in the case of shipwrecks, the Protection of Wrecks Act of 1973 empowers the Board of Trade to set up appropriate protection of any important sea-bed site and allow only approved individuals to work on it. Among many other countries, Italy and Greece have similar safeguards.

If an individual has a genuine interest in finding some ancient shipwreck or buried treasure he or she should not necessarily be disheartened by such legal constraints. As recorded by the initiator of the *Mary Rose* project, Alexander McKee, the Board of Trade in Whitehall granted him and his colleagues the licence to excavate the particular area of sea-bed where they thought the *Mary Rose* to be for an annual rent of precisely £1, scarcely a punitive amount. The laws of impounding recovered objects were eased so that these could be given appropriate conservation treatment, and in general there was little 'red tape' delay.

The important feature is that while anyone who has formulated an ambition to re-discover some ancient site or wreck may not be a professional himself, he should enlist the help of those who are, and keep on enlisting until it is obvious that the expertise brought to the project is at least worthy of the historical value of the anticipated find.

With these recommendations firmly in mind, what follows is just a taste of the fascinating world of lost cities, unlocated tombs, undiscovered shipwrecks, and occasional treasures that may reasonably be believed to be lying somewhere in the world, waiting for someone to turn them up. Anyone motivated to search for an item in *Undiscovered* will need patience, a sense for the past, and, not least, a fair share of luck. But given the technological resources of exploration now available, never have the opportunities been greater.

Part I
Undiscovered Places

*Surprising as it may seem, there remain 'lost' towns and
ancient locations waiting to be found even on an island
as well explored as Britain. Further afield, the
opportunities are even greater. But the uncovering of an
ancient location does not necessarily need expensive
technology or hacking one's way through a tropical
jungle. As we are about to see, a simple template applied to
a map may have identified where the Gauls fought their
last stand against the might of Julius Caesar. The long-
standing mystery of the whereabouts of King Arthur's battle
of Badon may be nearing solution thanks to an almost
elementary study of place-names. The number of ways to
discover a lost place can be as diverse as the places
themselves.*

THE BIBLICAL CITIES OF SODOM AND GOMORRAH

In the Bible the book of Genesis tells us that at the time of the patriarch Abraham, who is generally thought to have lived in the first half of the second millenium BC, there were two 'cities of the Plain', Sodom and Gomorrah. The male inhabitants of these cities were notorious for their homosexuality, but retribution awaited them. In the words of Genesis chapter 19: '. . . the Lord rained down fire and brimstone from the skies on Sodom and Gomorrah. He overthrew those cities and destroyed all the Plain, with everyone living there, and everything growing in the ground.'

The kings of Sodom and Gomorrah were apparently called Bera and Birsha (see Genesis chapter 14), and we are also told that the cities were 'in the valley of Siddim', that is the Salt, or Dead Sea. That some form of seismic catastrophe may have overwhelmed part of this region is in fact very credible, because it happens to lie on a major fault line in the earth's crust stretching from the Taurus Mountains in the north to as far as Lake Victoria in central Africa. So possibly Sodom and Gomorrah were located somewhere in this region, and were obliterated in the course of an earthquake, in which case their remains might somewhere be retrievable. Clearly, if they could be found the very suddenness of the catastrophe that overwhelmed them might have preserved insights on life in the Early Bronze Age as detailed as those of Pompeii and Herculaneum for the Roman period.

But can these 'lost cities' be located? There are a variety of clues which suggest that they can. Geologically, the Dead Sea is an extremely deep and relatively recent gash in the earth's surface, the water level being 1,292 feet below the nearby Mediterranean sea level, and its bed in the main northern section 1,000 feet below that. But near the southern end the Dead Sea's continuity is interrupted by a peninsula, El Lisan, which rises 50 to 140 feet above water level. To the south of this systematic soundings made in the nineteenth century indicate a depth of no more than six to eighteen feet. There are places where ancient tree trunks can be glimpsed beneath the waters, and it is generally agreed that this plain or plateau portion of the Dead Sea must have been land within historical times, with some of the submersion having been within the last hundred years. So could this have been the region of the biblical 'cities of the plain'?

Such a possibility assumes increasing significance when we note a particularly striking geological feature just to the west of this shallow portion of the Dead Sea, a hill five miles long, three miles wide, and over 700 feet high known as the Jebel Usdum. As determined by geologists, the lower portions of this are substantially composed of rock salt, deeply eroded, caverned and creviced, and liable to form

Facing page: Where biblical Sodom and Gomorrah might lie immersed beneath the Dead Sea? How the southern part of the Dead Sea includes former dry land that could have been 'the plain' of Genesis, chapter 14.

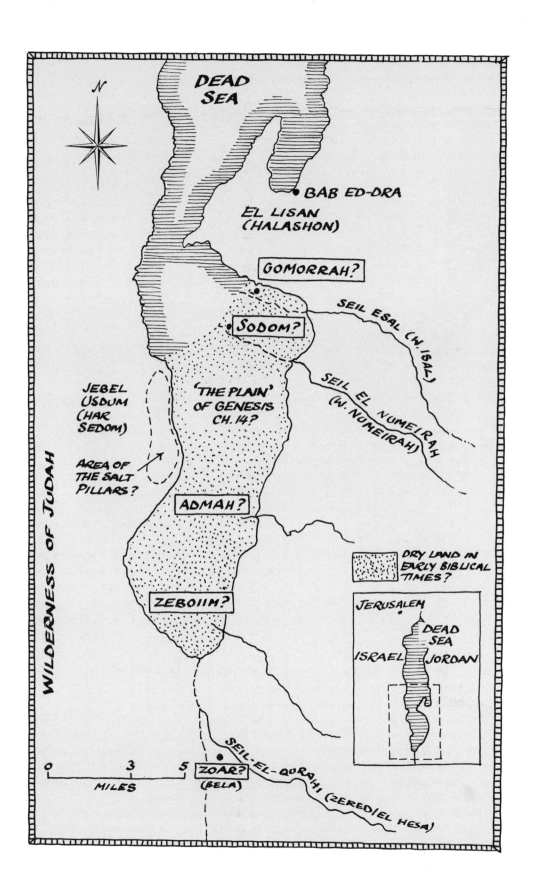

DEAD
SEA

• BAB ED-DRA

EL LISAN
(HALASHON)

GOMORRAH?

SEIL ESAL (W. ISAL)

SODOM?

SEIL EL NUMEIRAH
(W. NUMEIRAH)

JEBEL
USDUM
(HAR
SEDOM)

'THE PLAIN'
OF GENESIS
CH. 14?

AREA OF
THE SALT
PILLARS?

ADMAH?

WILDERNESS OF JUDAH

DRY LAND IN
EARLY BIBLICAL
TIMES?

ZEBOIIM?

JERUSALEM

DEAD
SEA

ISRAEL   JORDAN

0   3   5
MILES

ZOAR?
(BELA)

SEIL-EL-QURAHI (ZERED/EL HESA)

The origin of the biblical story of Lot's wife? One of the salt pillars in the Usdum region overlooking the Dead Sea

'pillars'. One of the first modern individuals to note this sort of feature in the vicinity of Usdum was the nineteenth-century American naval surveyor William Francis Lynch, who made a careful scientific exploration of the region in 1848:

> . . . to our astonishment, we saw on the eastern side of Usdum, one third of the distance from its north extreme, a lofty, round pillar, standing apparently detached from the general mass. . . . We found the pillar to be of solid salt, capped with carbonate of lime, cylindrical in front and pyramidical behind. The upper or rounded part is about forty feet high, resting on a kind of oval pedestal, from forty to sixty feet above the level of the sea. It slightly decreases in size upwards, crumbles at the top, and is one entire mass of crystallization. A prop, or buttress, connects it with the mountain behind. Its peculiar shape is doubtless attributable to the action of the winter rains.

Immediately to be recalled is the striking biblical story, during the escape from the destruction of Sodom and Gomorrah, of the turning of Lot's wife into a 'pillar of salt' (Genesis 19:26). Not only are the claims of subsequent early writers to have seen this pillar – among these Josephus, Clement of Rome and Irenaeus – therefore readily to be believed, what is also apparent from geological reports is that the exposure of this salt must have occurred within geologically recent times. The salt dome movement involved might therefore very credibly have happened at the same time as whatever seismic disaster was responsible for the destruction of Sodom and Gomorrah, accordingly, giving us a further reason for locating these cities in the southern portion of the Dead Sea.

But are we able to narrow their location even further? As it happens, Genesis chapter 14 mentions that besides Sodom and Gomorrah, there were three other 'cities of the Plain', Zoar, Admah and Zeboiim. The Dead Sea is, of course, extremely salty and quite undrinkable, and to support sizeable populations each of the cities of the Plain must therefore have needed proper sources of fresh water in reasonable abundance. In this context five freshwater streams happen to descend from the mountains of Moab into the Dead Sea in precisely the favoured shallower area. Since in the lists of the towns Sodom is mentioned first, arguably it was the biggest, and lay at the mouth of the most abundant stream, the Seil el Numeirah, while Gomorrah most likely lay to the north, on the banks of the Seil Esal. By the same reasoning biblical Zoar would have been on the Seil el-Qurahi, or river Zered, not far from the known Zoar of the Byzantine-Arabic period and Segor of the Middle Ages, while Admah and Zeboiim would have been on the remaining two streams.

In fact, clear evidence that this south-eastern sector of the Dead Sea was occupied in the Early Bronze Age has been quite evident from excavations carried out at a nearby hill called Bab ed-Dra. Here, during the 1920s the Jesuit Father Alexis Mallon, together with the American archaeologist Professor William Albright, brought to light a great fortress with 12-foot thick and 15-foot high walls encircling a settlement containing a series of seven fallen monoliths and great quantities of 'characteristically Early Bronze' pottery. As deduced by Albright, during the Early Bronze Age Bab ed-Dra had been a cult centre for the region, to which annual pilgrimages were most likely made by the inhabitants of towns 'now covered by the waters of the Dead Sea' (i.e. Sodom and Gomorrah and their neighbours). Furthermore, instead of having been overcome during some military conquest, Bab ed-Dra seems to have been suddenly abandoned at about the very same time that Sodom and Gomorrah would seem to have met their fiery fate.

What of the 'fire and brimstone' by which Sodom and Gomorrah are biblically described as having been destroyed? While the immediate impression this gives is of material thrown from a volcano, and there is a volcanic vent that has been noted by geologists in the eastern wall of the Dead Sea near the mouth of the Zerqa Ma'in, it is generally agreed that there has been no specific volcanic activity within the Dead Sea region during historical times.

However, as already noted, earthquakes are common in the area, and during these there can often be powerful exudations of bitumen, petroleum and natural gas, any of which, catching fire, would readily account for the description in the Bible. There are voluminous asphalt or bitumen deposits in the Wadi Mahawuat, about a mile west of Jebel Usdum, and since in ancient times the 'Vale of Siddim' is described as having been full of bituminous wells – which are no longer apparent now – the likely explanation is that these lay in the southern portion of the Dead Sea now underwater. Such an interpretation is supported by the fact that authors of the classical period, such as Diodorus Siculus, Josephus and Tacitus described bitumen rising to the surface of the Dead Sea in black and bulky masses. In 1834 after an earthquake so much of this material is reported to have come to the surface near the southern end of the Dead Sea, that according to the mid-nineteenth-century geologist Edward Hitchcock 'Arabs brought about six thousands pounds to market'. And during the present century raft-size lumps of bitumen have been noted and photographed floating in the southern Dead Sea. Accordingly, if there is any truth in the story of a lost Sodom and Gomorrah, it is in this area that they are most likely to be found.

With all the latest techniques of underwater exploration and recovery, might it therefore be possible to relocate and excavate ancient Sodom and Gomorrah? Although theoretically this should be so, in practice such an undertaking would have its own special difficulties, particularly due to the Dead Sea's exceptional salt content, five times that of any normal ocean. For underwater divers the high density of the water would mean a far greater consumption of air than normal, markedly reducing the length of any individual's time spent underwater. And the Dead Sea's extreme buoyancy would require each diver to wear very heavy lead weights as sinkers. These would need to be very carefully designed for gradual release, in order to avoid the danger of divers shooting to the surface before they have had a chance to empty their over-expanded lungs.

So, any expedition minded to find Sodom and Gomorrah would require to develop its own special techniques to overcome these and related hazards. And no one can tell how much four thousand years of seismic activity may have put any surviving remains beyond practical reach.

SOURCES:

The Bible, *Genesis* chapters 14, 18 and 19

JOSEPHUS, *Antiquities of the Jews*, I, chapter 11

ALBRIGHT, W. F., 'The Archaeological Results of an Expedition to Moab and the Dead Sea', *Bulletin of the American Schools of Oriental Research*, 14, 1924, pp. 2-12

—, 'The Jordan Valley in the Bronze Age', *Annual of the American Schools of Oriental Research*, 6, 1926, pp. 58-61

CLAPP, F. G., 'The Site of Sodom and Gomorrah', *American Journal of Archaeology*, vol. XL, 1925

HARLAND, J. P., 'Sodom and Gomorrah', *Biblical Archaeology*, vol. V, 1942, and vol. VI, 1943

HITCHCOCK, Edward, 'Notes on the Geology of Several Parts of Western Asia, Founded Chiefly on Specimens and Descriptions from American Missionaries'. *Transactions of the Association of American Geologists*, 1840-42, pp. 348-421

LYNCH, W. F., *Official Report of the United States' Expedition to Explore the Dead Sea and the River Jordan,* Baltimore, 1852

KYLE, M. G., *Explorations at Sodom*, London, Robert Scott, 1928

MOLYNEUX, Lieutenant William, 'Expedition to the Jordan and the Dead Sea', *Journal of the Royal Geographical Society*, vol. 18, 1848

WELLARD, James, *The Search for Lost Cities*, London, Constable, 1980

THE LOST LAND OF ATLANTIS

 In any discussion of undiscovered places, almost certainly the first name to come to mind, at least outside scholarly circles, is that of Atlantis, the so-called lost continent. Yet by any rational standards the Atlantis legend is one of the world's tallest stories. The fourth-century Athenian philosopher Plato first set it down in two of his dialogues, *Timaeus* and *Critias*, the Athenian Critias in these telling the tale as one which he had heard from his grandfather, who had in turn heard it from the sixth-century sage Solon. Solon in his turn was said to have heard it from Egyptian priests for whom it had happened a very long time ago, and very far away.

In his *Timaeus* the version that Plato puts into the mouth of the Egyptian priest is as follows:

Many great and wonderful deeds are recorded of your state [Athens] in our histories. But one of them exceeds all the rest in greatness and valour. For these histories tell of a mighty power which unprovoked made an expedition against the whole of Europe and Asia, and to which your city put an end. This power came forth out of the Atlantic Ocean, for in those days the Atlantic was navigable; and there was an island situated in front of the straits which are by you called the pillars of Heracles; the island was larger than Libya and Asia put together, and was the way to other islands, and from these you might pass to the whole of the opposite continent which surrounded the true ocean; for this sea which is within the Straits of Heracles [i.e. the Mediterranean] is only a harbour, having a narrow entrance, but that other is a real sea, and the land surrounding it on every side may be most truly called a boundless continent. Now in this island of Atlantis there was a great and wonderful empire which had rule over the whole island and several others, and over parts of the continent, and furthermore, the men of Atlantis had subjected the parts of Libya within the columns of Heracles [the straits of Gibraltar] as far as Egypt, and of Europe as far as Tyrrhenia [Etruria in north Italy]. This vast power, gathered into one, endeavoured to subdue at a blow our country and yours and the whole of the region within the straits; and then ... your country [Solon's city state of Athens] ... defeated and triumphed over the invaders, and preserved from slavery those who were not yet subjugated, and generously liberated all the rest of us who dwelt within the pillars. But afterwards here occurred violent earthquakes and floods; and in a single day and night of misfortune all your warlike men in a body sank into the earth, and the island of Atlantis in like manner disappeared in the depths of the sea.

In his second dialogue, *Critias* Plato described this ill-fated island of Atlantis in considerably expanded detail. In shape it was circular, with as its focal point an acropolis or hill where stood the royal palace, 'a marvel to behold for size and beauty', and notable for hot and cold water plumbing. Here, there ruled kings who at certain prescribed times hunted bulls that were allowed to roam freely in the temple precinct. These had to be captured without the aid of weapons, then sacrificed before a sacred pillar, after which there was feasting, and then the passing

of laws. During the law-giving the kings would dress in special azure robes. In the environs of the palace were temples for Atlantis's god Poseidon and his mistress Cleito, after whose son Atlas the island received its name. Both temples were rich in gold, silver, ivory and a metal which Plato called orichalcum. Walls and an inner harbour surrounded the central area, around which there was a ring of land, then a second harbour and a large outer circle of land featuring a well-irrigated plain with mountains to the north. One notable amenity was a racecourse for horses.

According to Plato Atlantis met its fate some eight or nine thousand years before the time of Solon (who lived *c.*600 BC), and on the basis of this information alone many distinguished Victorian classical scholars dismissed the tale as nothing more

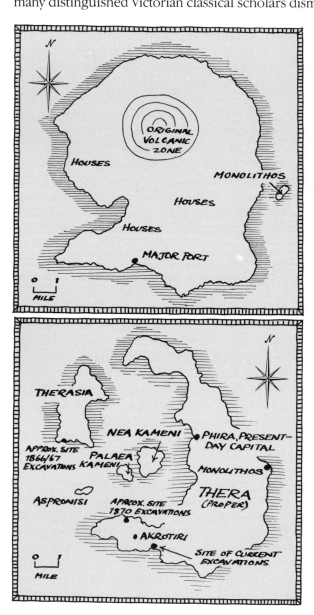

The origin of Plato's story of lost Atlantis? LEFT: A very approximate reconstruction of the shape of the Aegean volcanic island of Thera as it may have looked before the cataclysmic eruption of c.1500 BC. Houses are marked where remains have been found, but undoubtedly much, much more still lies buried beneath the pumice.

BELOW LEFT: The Thera island group as it looks today, showing how the original near-circular single island has splintered into three fragments, Therasia, Aspronisi and Thera itself, surrounding the now water-filled bay representing the site of the original volcanic caldera or crater. The 'burnt' islands of Palaea and Nea Kameni have been formed since the original eruption (the latter as recently as 1707), and remain volcanically active.

than a piece of make-believe, a romantic pipe-dream along the lines of Sir Thomas More's Utopia. But there were others in the nineteenth century who took it altogether more seriously, notably the American congressman Ignatius Donnelly who in a book called *Atlantis: the Antediluvian World* argued that there really was a lost continent west of the Straits of Gibraltar which perished in the circumstances Plato described. For Donnelly Atlantis was the cradle of civilized mankind, the missing link between the great cultures of the Old and New Worlds. The people of lost Atlantis invented the alphabet, developed the art of metallurgy, and much else.

When Donnelly was writing there was not much known about the geology of the Atlantic, and during the 1920s further fuel was provided for his theories by a writer called Lewis Spence. Aware that scholars were divided at that time on the origins of the mid-Atlantic ridge, an underwater mountain chain that stretches southwards from Iceland, Spence argued that this is a surviving part of what were originally two huge stepping stones across the Atlantic, 'Antilla', whose remains are the present-day West Indies, and 'Atlantis,' just to the west of Spain, which sank about 10,000 BC. While in Spence's time such a view could not be considered totally beyond the bounds of scientific possibility, it is today, now that geologists have reached a much better understanding of the formation of the earth's crust. Essentially, far from the mid-Atlantic ridge being the remains of a sunken continent, it is now recognized as being a very new geological development, formed by seismic forces which are causing it to rise above the rest of the Atlantic sea-bed.

But is Plato's story necessarily totally a piece of fiction? If his chronology and geographical setting are adhered to, then the answer is undoubtedly yes. Neither archaeologically nor geologically is there any justification for some lost 'stepping stone' between the Old and New Worlds around 10,000 BC. But if it is accepted that the lost land may not have been in the Atlantic, and that the disaster in which it sank may have happened not nine thousand, but nine hundred years before the time of Solon, then some greater credence to the story, as at least the glimmering of a memory of a real event, is possible.

For, in the midst of any number of theories of where the original Atlantis may have been – in South Africa, Sri Lanka, Brazil, Greenland, Mexico, the British Isles, Iran, Iraq and the Sahara, to name but a few – in 1909 the Irish scholar K. T. Frost suggested that the real Atlantis may have been the Minoan civilization of Crete, which undoubtedly suffered a sudden and rather mysterious eclipse about 1500 BC. According to Frost there was more than likely a language difficulty between the Greek Solon and the Egyptian priests from whom he learned the Atlantis story. When they spoke of a great island far to the west, they, untravelled in the Mediterranean, may only have intended to mean somewhere as near as Crete, while Solon, for whom Crete was on the doorstep, may have assumed that they must mean somewhere beyond the Straits of Gibraltar. Adding credence to this idea is the fact that the Egyptian name for the Cretans and their neighbours was *Keftiu*, which (broadly) means 'people of the pillar', and among the Greeks Atlas was the god who holds up the pillars of the sky, hence Atlantis, land of Atlas. The bull and pillar cult said to have been practised on Atlantis also have significant affinities to the near-identical cults practised on Minoan Crete.

Plausible as this might seem, it suffers from two serious flaws. First, Crete could never even remotely be considered a round island. Second, there is no evidence for

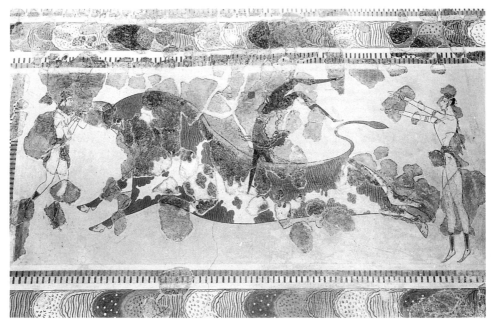

Plato described the Atlanteans practising a weaponless sport with bulls. Is this the memory of a Theran cult similar to the famous bull-leaping of nearby Minoan Crete?

Crete ever having disappeared 'in the depths of the sea' 'in a single day and night of misfortune', the central feature of the Atlantis story.

But both these objections can be dispelled at a stroke if, instead of Crete, the lost island is identified as Thera (or modern-day Thíra or Santorini) just sixty miles to Crete's north, and once featuring the same Minoan-style of civilization. Although today Thera is represented by a group of islands, Aspronisi, Therasia, and Thera proper, all circling a central bay, these are but the fragments of what was a single, indisputedly round island which blew apart in a massive volcanic eruption about 1500 BC. Geologically, it has been established that during this cataclysm the central part of the original island sank into the sea to form the present-day bay, and huge waves from underwater shocks during the same volcanic disturbances may well have caused the simultaneous flooding on the Greek mainland which Plato mentioned in the passage from *Timaeus*.

So colossal was the eruption that to this day much of Thera is covered by a huge layer of volcanic ash sometimes more than 100 feet deep. When during the nineteenth century massive amounts of this ash were used to supply cement for the Suez canal, occasional Minoan period remains were found, as a result of which in 1967 a Greek archaeologist, the late Professor Spyridon Marinatos began excavations at Akrotiri, in the south west of Thera proper, where the ash layer is thinner than elsewhere. Almost immediately Marinatos came across well-preserved remains of Minoan period houses featuring sophisticated plumbing systems, and beautifully decorated with frescoes depicting the Therans (or whatever name they were known by) living at a very advanced state of civilization. One fresco seems to be a depiction, prior to the eruption, of the original Theran seaport which the excavations are uncovering, and the discovery of a pair of so-called 'horns of consecration' shows that the Therans, like the Cretan Minoans, had a cult of the bull. Several of the houses show signs of having been damaged by an earthquake a significant period before being overwhelmed by the eruption, and from this and other evidence, notably the absence of household valuables and of human remains, it would appear that the earthquake acted as a warning to Thera's inhabitants to evacuate their island, and that they therefore managed to make a timely escape from what would otherwise have been certain destruction.

Professor Marinatos died in 1974, to be succeeded by another Greek, Professor Christos Doumas, who every year has painstakingly excavated further into the Akrotiri pumice, revealing more than a whole street of well-to-do houses. It is now clear that this particular site was a flourishing port, the full extent of which has yet to be uncovered in any direction. From miscellaneous, poorly recorded Minoan remains found on other parts of Thera and on Therasia, it is also quite evident that there were other substantial settlements elsewhere on the original single island, giving rise to the question of where might lie the remains of the island's royal palace (to be expected from the Minoan period examples found at Knossos and elsewhere on Crete), and any of its temples? If Thera was genuinely Plato's Atlantis, which reputedly had its palace and main temples on a high point in the centre of the island, then these would almost certainly have been on the original volcanic cone blown to

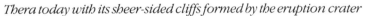

Thera today with its sheer-sided cliffs formed by the eruption crater

smithereens at the climax of the eruption. There is no reason why the Therans should have seen any danger building on the volcanic cone since it is geologically certain that the volcano had previously been inactive for many thousands of years.

So we may never know if Thera once had a palace and temples matching the description of Plato's Atlantis. The question of whether Plato's story was anything other than just a very tall story must therefore remain wide open. At the very least it had large factual inaccuracies, Thera in no way ever having been an island on the scale envisaged by Plato, nor in the place he imagined it, nor was it destroyed at anything like the time he thought.

But in fact, quite aside from any Atlantis connection Thera has a legitimate place in *Undiscovered* in its own right. For there are many, many more Minoan-period remains lying beneath the island's layers of ash, so much so that Professor Doumas estimates that at the present rate it may take more than a century to uncover the Akrotiri site alone. Because of the huge logistical problems involved, including the painstaking work restoring fresco paintings and the importance of the smallest minutiae of evidence, the uncovering of Thera must very rightly remain the preserve of the professional archaeologist, a role which Professor Doumas and his colleagues are fulfilling according to the very highest standards. But who knows what surprises – and possible further corroborations of the Atlantis story – their labours might any day reveal? Perhaps even a buried library of tablets that might provide the key to the still undeciphered Linear A script of Minoan Crete?

SOURCES:

JOWETT, B., *The Dialogues of Plato* (3rd ed.), Oxford, 1892, vol. 3

DONNELLY, Ignatius, *Atlantis: The Antediluvian World*, New York, 1882

DOUMAS, Christos G., *Thera, Pompeii of the Ancient Aegean*, London, Thames & Hudson, 1983

GALANOPOULOS, A. G. and E. Bacon, *Atlantis: The Truth behind the Legend*, London & New York, 1969

LUCE, J. V., *The End of Atlantis, New Light on an Old Legend*, London, Thames & Hudson, 1969

MARINATOS, S., 'The Volcanic Destruction of Minoan Crete', *Antiquity* 13, (1939), pp. 425-39

—, *Excavations at Thera*, 7 vols., Athens, 1967-73

RAMAGE, E. S., *Atlantis: Fact or Fiction?*, Bloomington, Indiana, 1979

SECOND INTERNATIONAL SCIENTIFIC CONFERENCE, *Thera and the Aegean World*, Papers and Proceedings of the Second International Scientific Congress, Santorini, Greece, August 1978, 2 vols., London, 1980

SPENCE, Lewis, *The Problem of Atlantis*, London, 1924

THE GREEK CITY OF HELIKE

In the second book of his *Iliad* the Greek poet Homer mentioned among those cities which provided forces for the famous expedition against Troy a particular one called Helike: 'Of them that possessed the . . . fortress of Mycenae . . . and dwelt about Aigion and through all the coastline and about broad Helike, of them did Lord Agamemnon son of Atreus lend an hundred ships . . .'

Regrettably, Homer gave no clear clue to Helike's location, but much later, in the second century AD, the traveller Pausanias provided further details in his *Description of Greece*:

> As you go on you come to the river Selinous, and about 40 stadia from Aigion is a place called Helike near the sea. It was once an important city, and the Ionians had there the most holy temple of Poseidon of Helike. The worship of Poseidon of Helike still remained with them, both when they were driven out by the Achaeans to Athens, and when they afterwards went from Athens to the maritime part of Asia Minor.
>
> And later on the Achaeans here, who drove some suppliants from the temple and slew them, met with quick vengeance from Poseidon, for an earthquake coming over the place rapidly overthrew all the buildings, and made the very site of the city difficult for posterity to find. . . .
>
> And they say another misfortune happened to the place in the winter at the

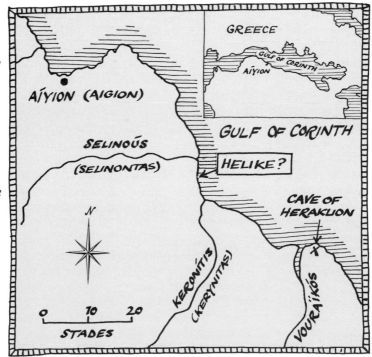

The site of Helike, one of the cities which contributed to the expeditionary forces which attacked Homer's Troy? Destroyed by earthquake and inundation in the 4th century BC, Helike, if found, could prove a Greek underwater equivalent of Pompeii.

same time. The sea encroached over much of the district and quite flooded Helike with water; and the grove of Poseidon was so submerged that the tops of the trees alone were visible. And so the god suddenly sending the earthquake, and the sea, encroaching simultaneously, the inundation swept away Helike and its population.

So Helike was suddenly erased from the map of Greece sometime before the time of Pausanias, but exactly when? The classical geographer Strabo (*c.*63 BC to after AD 21) stated that Helike was overwhelmed by waves 'two years before the battle of Leuktra', and since this famous battle between Thebans and Spartans is known to have taken place in 371 BC, the year of Helike's destruction seems to have been 373 BC, a dating loosely corroborated by another writer, Herakleidas of Pontus (*c.*322 BC) who stated that the catastrophe happened in his time. According to Strabo, a writer called Eratosthenes, who lived within two centuries of the destruction, described having been rowed by fishermen over the site where the city had been, on this occasion clearly seeing not only underwater ruins, but also a huge bronze statue of the god Poseidon, holding a sea-serpent.

Clearly then, if Helike could be rediscovered, it might provide at the very least a Greek underwater Pompeii of the fourth century BC. Since bronze statues are known to survive very well thousands of years immersion in the sea – as recently as 1972 two magnificent specimens were recovered from the sea off southern Italy – the possible additions to the world's collection of classical Greek art alone might well be dramatic. But from the information of Pausanias and others, can Helike be located? Surprisingly, it would seem that it can. The ancient Greek measure of distance, the stade, is known to have been equivalent to precisely 606¾ English feet, and we know from sources such as Pausanias that Helike was forty stades from Aigion and thirty stades from the Cave of Heraklion. Aigion is readily identifiable as the thriving present-day town of that name on the Gulf of Corinth, and since there is a Cave of Heraklion seventy stades to the south-east, a simple computation on a map shows that Helike would most likely have been at the mouth of the present-day rivers, Selinontas and Kerynitas. So why has not anyone found it so far, particularly with all the developments in underwater archaeology in recent years?

In fact, attempts have been made. In 1950 a French subaqua team, led by a dental surgeon, Dr Henri Chénevée and directed by the Hellenic scholar R. Demangel, made an exploration of the likely site, and found it, precisely because it is at the confluence of two rivers, to have accumulated heavy deposits of silt. A ship that had sunk as recently as the Second World War was found to be almost entirely covered by mud, indicating that anything of the fourth century BC was likely to be buried at depths quite impenetrable by the methods of the 1950s. A second attempt made in 1966 proved little more encouraging. But in the light of the recent *Mary Rose* discoveries the silt is in fact extraordinarily welcome news. It was the silt of the Solent which in the case of the *Mary Rose* acted virtually like embalming fluid on those organic remains it covered (see page 9), meaning that some quite unique insights into Greek life in the fourth century BC could await a Helike excavation of the future.

According to Demangel, Helike's ruins are likely to be between 550 and 1,600 yards from the present shoreline, covered by water between 50 and 130 feet deep, and an undetermined depth of mud. The well-respected British underwater archaeologist Dr Nicholas Flemming has offered a more conservative estimate, 20 feet of water plus an equal depth of mud. But until a fresh probe is made, requiring deployment of some of the silt-clearing techniques developed during the *Mary Rose* project, everyone is guessing. The bringing to light of fourth-century Helike would not be an undertaking for the amateur. After decisively identifying the location and determining its extent, almost certainly the best means of excavation would be to build a huge coffer dam around the area, pump the water out, then excavate as on land, an undertaking which would require very considerable financial backing. But Helike, as almost no other site, offers the opportunity of 'time-capsule' insights into the life of a suddenly snuffed out, bustling city of the Greek classical period, and it is to be hoped that someday the resources will be found.

One of the two magnificent Greek bronze statues found off southern Italy in 1972. Similar specimens from the high period of Greek art, plus possibly near-intact urban remains, could await anyone bold enough to try to recover the site of ancient Helike.

SOURCES:

HOMER, *Iliad* (trans. A. Lang, W. Leaf & E. Myers), London, Macmillan & Co, 1883, Book 2, v.569

CLEATOR, P. E., *Underwater Archaeology*, London, Robert Hale, 1973

DEACON, Sir George (ed.), *Oceans*, London, Paul Hamlyn, 1968 (Contribution by Dr N. C. Flemming)

PAUSANIAS, *Description of Greece*, London, Macmillan & Co, 1898

THE BATTLEFIELD OF ALESIA

English-speaking devotees of the ebulliant French strip cartoon characters, Astérix and Obélix are often unaware that the inspiration for these came from real-life heroes of ancient Gaul. Of these perhaps the most notable, if not the most easily pronounceable, was Vercingétorix, the French schoolboy's equivalent of England's Boudicca, or Boadicea. After Julius Caesar's ruthlessly efficient empire-building of the early fifties BC, during which Gallia or Gaul had been almost completely subjugated, it was Vercingétorix, son of a deposed chieftain from the Auvergne, who rose in revolt, by force of example and strong discipline inspiring the leaders of tribe after tribe to join him.

Back in Italy Caesar was obliged to gather a strong force to try to recover the lost territory, finding this by no means as easy as his original conquest. At a special convention held at Bibracte, near Autun, in 52 BC the Gaulish tribes near-unanimously hailed Vercingétorix as their supreme commander-in-chief, and then shortly after hurled their cavalry at Caesar's troops in a fierce engagement in which each man had been sworn not to return to his family unless he had broken through the Roman lines at least twice. Although the Gauls lost this engagement Vercingétorix prudently withdrew them to the fortress-town of Alesia, knowing this to be so readily defensible that here his men could withstand almost any attack, even from the ingenious Romans.

However, in Julius Caesar he was up against a commander of world-class tactical brilliance. Instead of attacking Alesia Caesar set about besieging it, confident that with some 80,000 men cooped up in the fortress Vercingétorix's food supplies would soon begin to fail. Anticipating this, Vercingétorix first sent some of his cavalry to try to break up the Roman entrenchment work, then, when this failed, gave the survivors the special mission of riding to all the friendly neighbouring Gaulish tribes to summon reinforcements, the deadline for these being the thirty days that he knew Alesia's food stocks could hold out.

Learning from captives that this was Vercingétorix's plan, Caesar and his men were now in a precarious position. The force within Alesia was still formidable, and if reinforcements came from a different direction the Romans could find themselves being attacked from two sides, with every danger of being overwhelmed. But, instead of contemplating withdrawal, Caesar coolly made his preparations for just such an emergency, setting his engineers to constructing two parallel lines of defences, each cunningly consisting partly of trenches, some filled with diverted river water, others with sharpened stakes, and partly of earthworks and battlements, from which the Roman firepower could be rained down on any number of attackers. Foraging was put in hand to ensure none of the Gaulish problem of inadequate food supplies.

For their part Vercingétorix's horsemen did not shirk their rallying of reinforcements, mustering a force of a quarter of a million, together with 8,000 cavalry, which in little more than the required thirty days arrived on the plain in front of Alesia, within sight of their compatriots high in the fortress, and no more than a mile from the Roman position. But the Romans, with an accompanying force of Germans, proved more than a match even for such a huge force of enemy. Despite some clever tactics by Vercingétorix and his allies, including carefully synchronized sallies against Roman weak-points, and use of hurdles to overcome the Roman trenches, Caesar set himself at a vantage point where he could quickly arrange reinforcements for any position in serious danger, at the most crucial point perso-

ABOVE: *Julius Caesar, victor of the Battle of Alesia. Was his memory of the battlefield faulty? Or did he describe a different location to the currently accepted site?*

LEFT: *The Gaulish leader Vercingétorix, loser of the Battle of Alesia. From the nineteenth-century statue that overlooks the supposed site at the village of Alise-Sainte-Reine*

nally entering the fray at the head of his most seasoned troop of cavalry.

The result was a rout in which, with the death or capture of the leaders of the reinforcements, seventy-four Gaulish war-standards taken, and Alesia's food stocks all but exhausted, Vercingétorix saw no option but surrender, being taken to captivity in Rome where after six years of solitary confinement he was brought out for Caesar's triumphal procession, then ignominiously executed.

By such feats, which he personally chronicled in his *De Bello Gallico (The Gallic War)* Caesar ensured his successful transformation of Rome from republic to dictator-controlled empire. Never again, during the five subsequent centuries would Gaul dare to challenge Rome's might.

Not least of the remarkable features of the battle of Alesia is that had Caesar lost – as he told his own troops, 'the fruit of all previous engagements depended upon that day and hour' – almost all of subsequent European history might have been quite different, with Britain, perhaps, remaining under the control of its native Celtic tribes who were blood brothers of Vercingétorix and his Gauls. Given the detailed description of the battle that has survived from Caesar, and the geography of the terrain that was so crucial to its outcome, an interesting question is therefore exactly where it may have occurred. Officially, as one learns from most classical histories, this is not in doubt.

In the Burgundian district of east-central France lies the village of Alise-Sainte-Reine, commanded by the distinctive plateau of Mont Auxois, and here in 1839 a French antiquary by the name of Maillard de Chambure unearthed a votive stone tablet carrying the Romano-Celtic inscription 'Martialis, son of Dannatalos, erected this building for Ucuetis [god of bronze-workers], Ucuetis *in Alisiia*'. In Alisia. Surely, if this was the name of the place in Roman times, then Mont Auxois must have been the Alesian stronghold where Vercingétorix made his last stand, the nearby plain being that where Caesar pitched his camp and fought so determinedly against the Gaulish cavalry? Little more than twenty years later such an identification received further support when a French farmer, digging on the plain, unearthed a cache of ancient weapons supposed to have been left over from after the battle.

Such discoveries were music to the ears of French emperor Napoleon III, at that time in the process of compiling a propagandist history of Julius Caesar's campaigns in ancient Gaul. In 1861 he commissioned large-scale excavations to commence around Alise-Sainte-Reine, when these proved initially unproductive sending in an artillery officer called Colonel Stoffel to speed up the work. In suitably double-quick time Stoffel not only produced an impressive haul of ancient coins and weapons but also claimed the discovery of Julius Caesar's original defence ditches, the earth in these apparently still so loose 'that even now after the lapse of 2,000 years it easily crumbles under the blows of the pick'.

It was all that Napoleon III needed. In 1865 a horse-drawn waggon trundled south from Paris carrying a huge statue of Vercingétorix with features flatteringly modelled in the emperor's own likeness, except that the Gallic nose suffered a little along the way from an unfortunate encounter with telegraph wires. After hurried re-modelling Vercingétorix was solemnly hauled upright on Mont Auxois to a commanding position overlooking the new Paris-Dijon railway line, the nearest railway station, with obvious appropriateness, duly receiving the name 'Les Laumes-Alésia'. Alise-Sainte-Reine had become, quite unequivocally, the official site of

Vercingétorix's battle of Alesia.

But even in the 1860s when all this was happening there were voices of doubt that Burgundian Alise really was ancient Alesia. As pointed out by the Besançon architect Alphonse Delacroix, Alaise in his own *département* of Franche-Comté better suited Julius Caesar's description of the battleground. To Delacroix's support came, among others, the botanist Georges Colomb, a pioneer of the French comic strip from which, a century later, *Astérix the Gaul* would evolve. Excavations were tried at Alaise, but these did little to provide any support to the Franche-Comté cause.

Recently, however, there have been yet more powerful arguments against the Alise-Sainte-Reine identification. The question largely revolves around the accuracy of Julius Caesar's description of the terrain, something he should have known well as the success of his strategy was based on it. According to *De Bello Gallico*:

> The actual stronghold [*oppidum*] of Alesia was set atop of a hill, in a very lofty situation, apparently impregnable save by a blockade. The bases of the hill were washed on two separate sides by rivers. Before the town a plain extended for a length of about three miles; on all the other sides there were hills surrounding the town at a short distance, and equal to it in height.

As pointed out by the French archaeologist and palaeographer André Berthier, if Alise-Sainte-Reine's plateau of Mont Auxois was Vercingétorix's *oppidum* or citadel, it neither seems quite as lofty as suggested by Caesar nor big enough to cope with 80,000 Gallic warriors and their trappings during the required six-week period. The low land in front does not constitute a three-mile stretch of plain. Similarly, the streams of the Oze and Ozerain, while they border the territory, do not exactly wash the citadel's sides.

So what is Berthier's suggestion for the true site? His method for trying to pinpoint it has been both novel and interesting. Taking as his base that Caesar's description of Alesia is genuinely accurate he constructed a schematic tracing of what this should look like, then began moving this over 1:50,000-scale maps of all the most likely regions in France, including Alise-Sainte Reine, Alaise and various other contenders suggested in what has been a lively source of French debate since the late nineteenth century. Not one seemed to fit.

Then Berthier applied his tracing to Syam-Cornu, an area high in the Jura massif just a few miles south of Champagnole, and not far from the Swiss border. The match was remarkable. As he noted in the journal *Les Dossiers de l'Histoire*:

> Before our eyes we had a striking spur, remarkably cut off by a succession of hills in a perfectly straight line and forming the most powerful of natural walls.
>
> This fortified position was protected on its two sides by two rivers, the Lemme and the Seine, whose gorges created gigantic moats. In front stretched a little valley. As for the mountain to the north [a landmark singled out for special mention by Caesar], it was 'ready and waiting'. This recognition of a 'face' called for a whole series of tests. Measurements first of all. *Everything fitted*. The eleven-mile perimeter of the *oppidum* corresponded to the dimensions given by Caesar. The little valley was enclosed between hills and was exactly three miles long. The north mountain was massive from the outside.
> . . . It might have been predestined to receive the 60,000 assault troops of the Gaulish chief Vercassivellaunos.
>
> Where were we? The position . . . barred the line of retreat from Langres to

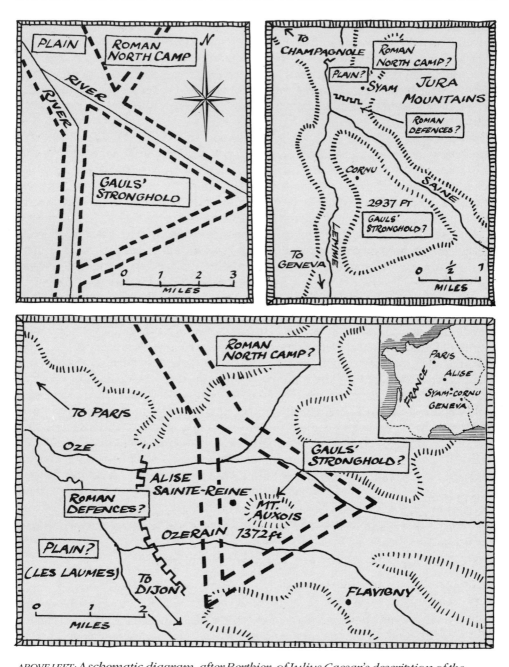

ABOVE LEFT: *A schematic diagram, after Berthier, of Julius Caesar's description of the battlefield of Alesia.* ABOVE RIGHT: *How this does fit the Syam-Cornu site near the Swiss border.* BELOW: *How this does not fit the traditionally accepted site at Alise-Sainte-Reine.*

Geneva, as it is determined by an objective analysis of the text in which Caesar describes how he is taking the 'easiest' route to avoid the mass of Gaulish troops and reach the land of the Allobroges, today's Savoy.

Berthier has attracted some distinguished support for his views, including the academic René Potier, who set it all down in a special thesis. In 1980 a society was formed – the Association Lemme et Saine d'Intérêt Archéologique, or ALESIA – specifically to search for any corroborative evidence at the Syam-Cornu site. Although so far they have been allowed to do little, they have already made some potentially significant finds, including part of an undoubted Roman *patera* or libation bowl.

But what of the cache of weapons found by the farmer on the plain of Alise-Sainte-Reine? These have been shown to be not of the right period. What of the various coins and military items excavated from Alise-Sainte-Reine by Colonel Stoffel? These are preserved to this day in the vaults of France's Museum of National Antiquities at Saint-Germain-en-Laye, just outside Paris, but insufficient access has been allowed for modern scholars to determine whether they might genuinely derive from the battle. Most problematic of all, what of the votive inscription found at Alise-Sainte-Reine, specifically indicating that this was known as *Alisiia* in Roman times? According to Berthier and his supporters, Roman Gaul more than likely had several Alisias, just as Britain has several Newports and the United States any number of Washingtons. Nonetheless, it is on this point that the Berthier argument is at its weakest. The Alise-Sainte-Reine site conforms sufficiently closely to Julius Caesar's description for the inscription/topography combination to remain compelling, albeit not conclusive. Berthier and his adherents have yet to find the sort of evidence that would cause books of classical history to be re-written.

So is Syam-Cornu the real site of Vercingétorix's last stand? Only some very thorough professional archaeological excavations both on this site and at Alise-Sainte-Reine (at least, what Colonel Stoffel's diggings left of it) are likely to provide the answer.

SOURCES:

CAESAR, Julius, *The Gallic War*, trans. H. J. Edwards, London, Heinemann, 1937, chapter 7

BERTHIER, André and others, articles in the July-August issue of *Les Dossiers de L'Histoire*, published by Les Editions de l'Université et de l'Enseignement Moderne, 25 rue Saint-Sulpice, 75006 Paris (translation of extract from this article derived from article by Malkin, listed below)

LE GALL, Prof. Joseph, *Alésia, Archéologie et Histoire*, Paris, Fayard, 1980

MALKIN, Roy, 'The Mystery of Alesia: Where was Vercingétorix's last stand?' *Popular Archaeology*, vol. 4, no. 6, December 1982, pp.22-27

POTIER, René, *Le Génie Militaire de Vercingétorix et le mythe Alise-Alesia*, Clermont Ferrand, Editions Volcans, 1973

POMPEII'S LOST NEIGHBOURS

Stadium riots such as that in which thirty-nine football fans were killed in Brussels in 1985 are not a phenomenon peculiar to the twentieth century. In AD 59 at the populous Roman port of Pompeii fights broke out among the crowd in the amphitheatre during a gladiatorial contest, an incident considered sufficiently serious that the Roman Senate subsequently banned all further amphitheatre shows at Pompeii for the next ten years.

Nor was this to be Pompeii's only taste of tragedy. On 5 February AD 62, an

The site of the Vesuvius eruption of AD 79. It is often supposed that only Pompeii and Herculaneum were overwhelmed. But Latin sources also indicate the loss of Sora, Tora, Taurania, Cossa and Leucopetra, places all unlocated so far.

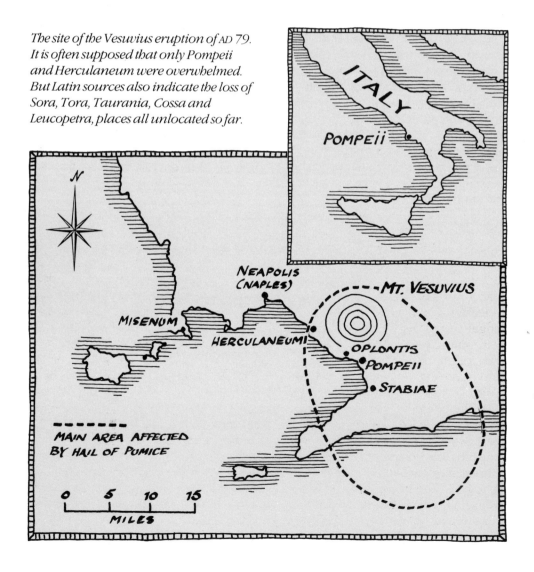

earthquake hit the town, damaging both public buildings and private houses so seriously that rebuilding work was still heavily in progress seventeen years later.

But, as is now a matter of history, this was merely the curtain-raiser to Pompeii's real disaster. For many centuries there had never been any trouble from the volcano Vesuvius, which dominated the horizon to Pompeii's north east. Villas and vineyards dotted its slopes, and it was universally thought to be extinct.

The shock was accordingly all the more severe when, between 10 and 11 o'clock on the morning of 24 August AD 79, Vesuvius sprang savagely back to life. At the time a Roman fleet under the command of the scientifically minded Pliny the Elder happened to be stationed at Misenum, nineteen miles to the west, and it was Pliny's nephew, Pliny the Younger, who lived to provide a graphic account of Vesuvius's volcanic cloud as he witnessed it about 1 pm that day:

> I cannot describe its appearance and shape better than as resembling an umbrella pine tree, with a very tall trunk rising high into the sky and then spreading out into branches. I imagine this was because where the force of the blast was fresh it thrust upwards, but as this lost impetus, or indeed as the weight of the cloud itself took charge, it began to thin out and to spread laterally. At one moment it was white, at another dark and dirty, as if it carried up a load of earth and cinders.

Throughout the next twenty-four hours and beyond Vesuvius spewed out a torrent of pumice and volcanic ash, accompanied by deadly, sulphurous fumes. Characteristically eager to be at the heart of any action, the elder Pliny took a ship towards Pompeii's well-to-do sister town of Herculaneum. Finding it impossible to land, he spent the night at a friend's coastal villa at Stabiae, to Pompeii's south. The next morning, trying to make for the beach to escape constantly falling ash, he was overcome by the fumes and died.

Meanwhile, Pompeii itself, slowly but inexorably smothered by some twelve feet of ash, had simply been blotted out of all further existence. Although many citizens had managed to escape out into the countryside, or to get away by sea, those who had not, or had chosen to seek refuge in subterranean rooms, were asphyxiated and entombed where they lay. At Herculaneum, where Pliny had been unable to land, the volcano first bombarded the town with incandescent pebbles and rocks, then released an avalanche of liquid mud so huge that in some places the streets were engulfed up to sixty-five feet deep, overcoming dozens of citizens waiting in the harbour for rescue. When some form of normality was restored the whole coastline was found to have been changed beyond recognition, and not only had Pompeii and Herculaneum been effaced, but also their neighbours, Stabiae, Oplontis, Sora, Tora, Taurania, Cossa and Leucopetra.

In the immediate aftermath, during which at Pompeii at least some of the upper parts of the more important buildings jutted above the ash layer, both thieves and past owners dug into the debris to retrieve bronze statuary, items of marble, and anything else of value that they could reach. Someone, perhaps a local Jew or Christian, scratched the words 'SODOM GOMORA' on a wall. The emperor Titus, who had been in command of the Empire for only six weeks, gave orders for the salvaging of some temple pictures and statuary. Then, particularly after outbreaks of plague and fire in Rome, the whole area that Vesuvius had devastated became overgrown and forgotten. By the eighteenth century all that remained was the

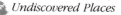

regional name Civita ('city') as a dim folk memory of what had once been.

Then, in 1710 the French aristocrat Emanuel-Maurice, Prince of Elbeuf, decided to build a small country house in the district. At about this same time a local peasant while digging a well came across some costly marbles, which a Frenchman employed by Elbeuf correctly recognized as having come from some obviously important ancient building. Excited, Elbeuf promptly bought the land surrounding the well, and paid workmen to dig deep underground channels from which more and more antiquities came to light. Although after a few years Elbeuf had to relinquish these antiquarian interests because of other responsibilities, around the middle of the eighteenth century, when the Pompeii region had become part of the realms of Charles, Bourbon king of Naples and Sicily, further excavations were carried out, this time with the help of gunpowder.

Now major statues and painted frescoes – the latter the first known examples from the Roman period – began to come to light, followed by a large and superbly appointed villa complete with a library of some 1,800 scrolls of papyri. Although at first no one could open these to read them because they simply crumbled at the slightest touch, an Augustinian called Father Piaggi found the right technique for unrolling them using a device similar to that with which wig-makers prepared hair. Sadly, for all his labours, the papyri turned out to be the works of very minor authors, of little interest, but a major conservation method had been pioneered.

It was now quite obvious that ancient Pompeii and Herculaneum had been found, and the first large folio report on the excavations was published at royal expense in 1757. But even to scholars of the time much of the work was being carried out very unscientifically, the actual excavators being galley-slaves working in underground conditions described by one English visitor as 'exactly like a coal mine'. There was also undue secrecy, prompted partly by the flagrantly erotic nature of some of the finds.

However, a century later, during the reign of Victor Emmanuel II of Savoy, a young and exceptionally scholarly excavator called Giuseppe Fiorelli was appointed. He instituted a proper plan of Pompeii divided into *insulae*, or sections, with each house given its own individual number. He launched a journal in which all new finds were to be recorded, together with their exact location, and any appropriate interpretations. He devised a plaster-cast system by which, when tell-tale cavities were found in the pumice, the exact time-of-death appearance of humans and animals killed in the eruptions could be retrieved. And he arranged that, so far as possible, all major objects and paintings should be left *in situ* rather than, as had happened previously, carted off to Naples or other museums.

Since Fiorelli successions of more recent excavations have opened up considerably more of Pompeii, together with such a wealth of artistic and everyday objects that it is possible to recapture a great deal of the flavour of Roman life of the first century AD. The finds include everything from the *lupanar* or brothel with its appropriately decorated walls, to a chained watch-dog frozen in his last agony, to the pathetic bodies of a farming family overcome in the very act of trying to flee for safety with their family valuables.

But if the opening-up of Pompeii has come relatively near to completion, this is not the case with Herculaneum, which, because the early, Bourbon-backed excavators did not push sufficiently far with their subterranean corridors under the streets

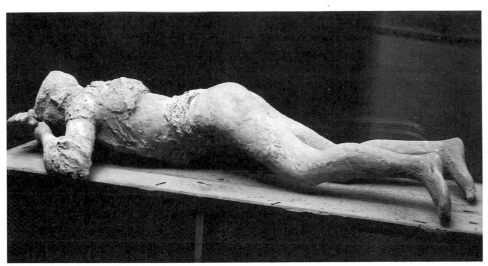

Frozen in time, the body of an asphyxiated Pompeiian girl perfectly cast by the hardening of the ash which entombed her

of Resina, has only fractionally been uncovered. That it must have had a population of some 4-5,000 is quite clear from, among other indications, the seating capacity of its theatre, and since in general the private houses appear to have been more well-to-do than at Pompeii there will almost certainly be other villas like that of the Papyri, and hopefully ones whose owners had more discriminating literary tastes. The prospect of priceless missing copies of works of classical authors lying possibly still well preserved beneath the streets of modern Resina is one that caused the English archaeologist Sir Charles Walston as long ago as 1904 to urge: 'Herculaneum is the one site above all others which ought to be excavated.'

In 1966 without anything having been done Walston's plea was taken up by the Yale University archaeologist Frank E. Brown: 'Herculaneum is probably archaeology's most flagrant unfinished business, . . . the incompleteness that the archaeologist must one day make good.'

As recently as 1985 the author Joseph Jay Deiss could only add to these pleas one of his own: 'So far as is known, nowhere else in all the world is such a time capsule waiting to be opened. Antiquity is Italy's greatest natural resource, Herculaneum the richest of all finds. It seems incredible and absurd to discover a buried treasure – and not dig it up.'

One inevitable problem is the existence of modern housing overlying much of where unexcavated Herculaneum is suspected to lie. But so far the authorities have shown no sign of restricting fresh urban development in the area, and much of the existing habitation is of such shoddy construction that relocation and rehousing of the population would scarcely be a social disaster.

However, even aside from Pompeii and Herculaneum, there were quite definitely other Roman centres of population overwhelmed by Vesuvius during the fatal August days of AD 79. One of these was Oplontis, which on a Roman map called the Peutinger Table, preserved in Vienna, is actually given greater prominence than the 'HERCULANIUM' and 'POMPEIS' shown, with correct distances between them, in the same district. The location of Oplontis was unknown until 1964, when at Torre Annunziata, three miles to the west of Pompeii, the Italian excavator Professor Alfonso De Franciscis discovered an opulent Roman seaside villa buried beneath fifteen feet of volcanic mud and some five feet of ash and pumice.

This magnificent villa, only the eastern half of which has been uncovered because the rest runs beneath a modern road, would seem to have been part of Oplontis, and to have been owned by Nero's wife Poppaea Sabina up to the time of her death in AD 65. It was then unoccupied for a while, and would seem to have been being redecorated for unknown new owners at the time the eruption struck. From a range of other classical antiquities that have from time to time been found at Torre Annunziata it is evident that Poppaea's villa is not all there was to Oplontis. There is likely to be at least one more similarly opulent villa waiting to be discovered.

Besides Oplontis, other places quite positively known from ancient sources to have been overwhelmed by the eruption of AD 79 are Sora, Tora, Taurania, Cossa, and Leucopetra. The location of none of these has yet been identified. It is anyone's guess how important any of them may have been, but it is at least significant that the younger Pliny, who did not specifically mention Pompeii and Herculaneum by name, spoke of the Vesuvius eruption having caused the destruction of 'so many populous cities' – suggesting that there could well be some substantial further discoveries yet to come.

The particularly exciting feature is that while so much of Pompeii suffered from the gun-powder-style excavation methods used during the eighteenth century – in the course of which an incalculable amount of valuable archaeological data will have been lost – any newly discovered cities could be opened with all the painstaking methods of the archaeology of the present day. And with the development of increasingly sophisticated methods of 'seeing' below the soil there is every prospect that one day Pompeii's lost neighbours will be relocated, undoubtedly adding immensely to our knowledge and appreciation of the classical past.

SOURCES:

DEISS, Joseph Jay, *Herculanaeum, Italy's Buried Treasure*, New York, Harper & Row, revised edition 1985

GRANT, Michael, *Cities of Vesuvius: Pompeii and Herculanaeum,* London, Penguin, 1976

TREVELYAN, Raleigh, *The Shadow of Vesuvius, Pompeii AD. 79*, London, Michael Joseph, 1976

WARD-PERKINS, John, and Amanda Claridge, *Pompeii AD. 79*, London, Royal Academy exhibition catalogue, 1976

THE BATTLEFIELD OF
MOUNT BADON

Among the many mysteries associated with England's semi-legendary King Arthur – not least of these whether he even existed (see 'The Grave of King of Arthur' page 73) – a prevailing source of controversy among scholars has been the location of his historically best attested battle, that of Mount Badon.

The first chronicler to make any mention of the occurrence of this battle was Gildas, a sixth-century native British monk thought to have lived and died at Glastonbury in Somerset. In his *De Excidio et Conquesti Britanniae*, an attempt at a history of Britain pre-AD 547, he gives a sketchy picture of the struggles of the Romano-British left to fend for themselves after the Roman withdrawal, culminating in a resounding victory for the native British against invading Anglo-Saxons at the siege of *Badonici montis*, or Mount Badon. The immediate problem is that although this battle seems to have been quite close to Gildas's own time, he says all

Controversy has raged for centuries over the location of King Arthur's famous battle of Mount Badon. Theories have ranged from as far afield as Scotland and France to Wiltshire and Dorset. But now some almost elementary place-name research suggests that it might have been fought on one of the hills surrounding Bath, possibly on soaring Lansdown Hill to the north of the city.

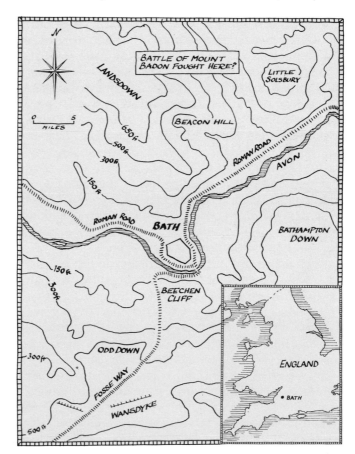

too little about it, providing neither the names of any leaders, nor any clue as to what part of the country *Badonici montis* might have been.

However, much later, in the ninth century a little more light is thrown by Nennius, a cleric in the household of the Bishop of Bangor in north Wales. In his *Historia Britonum*, which he is thought to have revised rather than initiated, he provides some fanciful stories associated with the immediate post-Roman period, then goes on to name for the first time the leader associated with the Badon victory:

> Arthur fought against the Saxons alongside the kings of the Britons, but he himself was the leader in the battles [in the original Latin, *dux bellorum*]. The first battle was at the mouth of the river which is called Glein. . . . The twelfth was on Mount Badon [*monte Badonis*], in which – on that one day – there fell in one onslaught of Arthur's nine hundred and sixty men; and none slew them but he alone, and in all his battles he remained victor.

Nennius may have used as his source documents now lost, but like Gildas, he fails to provide any location for the Badon battle, as if everyone would know where this was. Nonetheless, some further corroboration that Badon was a genuine historical event is provided by the tenth-century *Annales Cambriae*, the ancient Welsh annals, which enshrined the memories of the native Celtic Britons whom the invading Anglo-Saxons pushed into Wales and the west of England. These record as part of their listing of early events:

> 518 [AD]. The battle of Badon in which Arthur carried the cross of our Lord for three days and three nights on his shoulders, and the Britons were the victors.

It is not exactly a great deal of information, so given the obvious difficulties, where might this obviously crucial battle of Badon have taken place? For decades this has been a source of considerable mystery to scholars. One theory has placed the sites of all Arthur's battles, including Badon, in Scotland. Another has placed them in France. Because the Badon descriptions suggest a hill-fort some who have favoured setting Arthur in southern England have suggested Badbury Rings in Dorset, but this is unlikely because it is not strategic enough. More strongly tipped has been the 900-foot high 'Liddington Castle' ramparted earthwork just south of Swindon in Wiltshire, a by-no-means unreasonable candidate because it would have formed a natural command centre for the great Wansdyke earthwork believed to have been thrown up to hold back the Saxons by Arthur's likely predecessor, the immediate post-Roman leader Ambrosius Aurelianus. As the Wansdyke has been described by the author Geoffrey Ashe:

> Its impressive ditch and rampart run fifty miles from Inkpen through Saver-nake Forest, along the Marlborough Downs, past Bath and Stantonbury and thence brokenly to the Bristol Channel. It faces north, it belongs to the right period, and history records no other strategic situation which would account for it.

Furthermore, there is a 'Badbury' in the immediate vicinity, which has to be passed by every west-bound driver who skirts Swindon on the M4 motorway.

But is such an identification correct? And in particular, is there any way of locating the place-name 'Badon' with greater assurance, any such breakthrough promising to provide the folk-hero Arthur with a greater historical credibility than he enjoys at present? As it happens this may very recently have become possible, thanks not to any relevant fresh archaeological work (as yet), but to the delvings of two shrewd

Nennius' hot lake 'where the baths of Badon are'? Roman Bath's Great Bath today

researchers into place-names, Annette Bennett and Timothy Burkitt.

As Bennett and Burkitt have noted, in the works of Nennius the name 'Badonis' or Badon occurs not solely in respect of Arthur's battle. Nennius uses it again in the *De Mirabilus Britanniae* or 'Wonders of Britain' part of his history in which he describes as his third wonder the hot lake 'where the baths of Badon are'. This lake is specifically mentioned as in the territory of the Hwicce, a Mercian sub-tribe whose lands are known to have included present-day Bath. So, it would appear that for Nennius the 'baths of Badon' were one and the same as the magnificent baths which the Romans built over Bath's ancient hot springs – to this day one of Britain's major paying tourist attractions, second only to the Tower of London.

Now if Badon in this context was Bath of the Roman Baths, surely the site of the

Arthurian battle of Badon must similarly have been Bath? Indeed, given such an apparently reasonable identification, it is perhaps remarkable that such a suggestion should not have been put forward before. One source of uncertainty has lain in the fact that the normal Roman name for Bath – and the one which Nennius, writing in Latin, might have been expected to use – was *Aquae Sulis*, or 'Waters of Sulis', Sulis being the name the Celts gave to the goddess they believed responsible for the waters' remarkable properties. However, there is a perfectly straightforward explanation for this. Both Nennius and Gildas before him were undeniably Celtic British and did not have any particular affinity, save their use of Latin, to the world of Rome. They may well therefore have preferred to use what may now be inferred to have been Bath's original Celtic name, Badon, the significant point being – and few before Bennett and Burkitt seem to have appreciated this – that to this day in modern Welsh (the descendant of the language of the Celtic Britons) the word for bath is *baddon*, pronounced 'bathon'. So there is every reason to believe that this is how 'Badon', in respect of the battlefield, would have been pronounced back in King Arthur's sixth century. And in one of Bath's earliest documents, a list of the holy relics to be found at the city's Priory of St Peter, 'Badon' is used several times, followed in later documents by the variants 'Badan', 'Badaran', 'Bathe', and others.

So, was the semi-legendary Arthurian battle of Mount Badon a very real sixth-century historical battle for Bath? That sixth-century Bath was of some significant strategic importance seems quite clear from the fact that the Anglo-Saxon Chronicle records as a major event its capture in AD 577, there seeming to have been yet another struggle for the place in AD 665, since the *Annales Cambriae* records a second battle of Badon in that year. The reasonable inference is that the city, at an important junction of the Roman road network (it commanded the lateral Fosse Way and the route eastwards for Londinium), was a key rallying-point for those Britons who had been driven westward by the Saxon advance. A tentative reconstruction of events is that it held out under Arthur in 518 (if the *Annales Cambriae* date is to be believed), then succumbed in 577, was perhaps recaptured by the Britons shortly after, only to fall to the Saxons for the final time in AD 665. Thus, Bath rather than 'Liddington Castle' may have been the true control centre for the Wansdyke. And there may be no accident in the fact that one of the finest of surviving Anglo-Saxon poems, in describing the ruin of what seems specifically to have been Bath's earlier Roman glories, harps particularly on the city's fortifications:

> Bright were the castle-dwellings, many the bath-houses, lofty the host of pinnacles . . . till Fate the might overturned that. The wide walls fell; days of pestilence came; death swept away all the bravery of men; their fortresses became waste places; the city fell to ruin. . . . Wherefore these courts are in decay and these lofty gates; the woodwork of the roof is stripped of tiles; the place has sunk into ruin, levelled to the hills, where in times past many a man . . . gazed on treasure, on silver, on precious stones, on riches, on possessions, on costly gems, on this bright castle of the broad kingdom. Stone courts stood here; the stream with its great gush sprang forth hotly; the wall enclosed all within its bright bosom; there the baths were hot in its centre. . . .

But was Bath itself the *mons* or hill of the battle, or did the actual fighting occur on one of the several hills surrounding? According to an eighteenth-century Bath chronicler John Wood, one of these hills had in his time two alternative names –

Was Lansdown Hill outside Bath the site of King Arthur's battle?

Lansdown (the name it retains to the present day) and . . . *Mons Badonca*.

So, could there still survive beneath the soil of Lansdown Hill some of the discarded weapons of a fierce engagement between Romano-Britains under Arthur and invading Anglo-Saxons? Might there still be in the vicinity some cemetery where dead warriors from the battle – perhaps real-life knights of King Arthur – were laid to rest? Such questions are not ones to be settled by amateurs with metal-detectors; only some careful future archaeologial work is likely to provide the answers. But, at least, very largely thanks to Bennett and Burkitt's clever desk-research into place-names, it looks as if the mystery of the site of the battle of Mount Badon may no longer be quite such a mystery after all.

SOURCES:

The works of Gildas and Nennius, and the *Annales Cambriae* in editions by J. Morris, (ed.) Chichester 1978 & 1980

Anglo-Saxon poem 'The Ruin', from *Anglo-Saxon Poetry*, selected and translated by Prof. R. K. Gordon, London, Everyman, 1926, p. 84

ASHE, Geoffrey, *King Arthur's Avalon*, London, Collins, 1957

BENNETT, Annette, and Timothy Burkitt, 'Badon as Bath'. *Popular Archaeology*, vol. 6, no. 6, April 1985, pp. 6-8 including map

GARMONSWAY, G. N. *The Anglo-Saxon Chronicle*, Bungay, Suffolk, 1953

HUNT, W., 'Two chartularies of the Priory of St Peter at Bath', *Somerset Record Soc.* 1.7., 1983, pp. 6-7

WOOD, John, *Essay Towards a Description of Bath,* (1765), Kingsmead Reprints, Bath, 1969

Part II

Undiscovered Graves

As recently as 8 February 1986 the British Egyptologist,
Dr Geoffrey Martin and his Dutch colleague, Dr Jacobus
van Rijk, exploring a dusty tomb-shape at Saqqara,
rediscovered a tomb they had been trying to find for some
eleven years, that of Maya, one of the highest officials of the
pharaoh Tutankhamun. It was not a blind discovery.
Records of the pioneering nineteenth-century Prussian
Egyptologist, Richard Lepsius indicated that the tomb,
rifled in antiquity, but richly decorated, lay somewhere
among Saqqara's sprawling necropolis.

This is but one instance of how all over the world there are
burial and last resting places of great and famous persons
still waiting to be located or successfully unearthed.
Sometimes the problems are technical ones of access. In the
case of others it is a question of determining where best to
look. What follow are just some of the potentially
intriguing graves that have yet to be brought to light.

LOST TOMBS OF THE ANCIENT EGYPTIANS

Much as every present-day Egyptologist would like to unearth the intact tomb of a pharaoh, in practice most, if not all, recognize that there is unlikely ever to be any such discovery. The fact is that of the early pharaohs who chose to be buried in pyramids, the thorough looting of these in antiquity is plain for every visitor to Egypt to see. Surprisingly, despite their size not all pyramids have yet been uncovered from Egypt's sand. Somewhere at Saqqara, for instance, where Maya's tomb has so recently been found, must be the remains of a pyramid of the Fifth Dynasty pharaoh Menkauhor, mentioned in ancient texts as 'The Pyramid which is Divine of Places'; also one of the Seventh/Eighth Dynasty pharaoh Neferkare, known in antiquity as 'The Enduring and Living Pyramid'. Occasionally such 'lost' pyramids are uncovered, as in 1950, when the Egyptologist Zakaria Goneim brought to light an abandoned one of Sekhemkhet, successor to the Third Dynasty pharaoh Djoser. But it is unlikely that any future discovery of this kind will have gone undisturbed.

The same pessimism applies to those pharaohs from the Eighteenth Dynasty who, precisely because of the earlier lootings, tried to conceal their tombs from robbers in Thebes' now world-famous Valley of the Kings. A simple check between the list of pharaohs and those tombs already discovered in this Valley – all, with the exception of Tutankhamun's, more or less completely looted – reveals no great gaps for anyone of significance (see facing page).

In fact, it was predominantly because, prior to 1922, Tutankhamun's was the one glaring anomaly on this list (although an earlier excavator, Theodore Davis, had erroneously identified a small rock-cut tomb as Tutankhamun's), that the British Egyptologist Howard Carter and his patron Lord Carnarvon had high hopes of finding Tutankhamun's tomb and no other when their workers began digging an otherwise unprepossessing triangular area in the Valley of the Kings. In Carter's own words: 'At the risk of being accused of *post actum* prescience, I will state that we had definite hopes of finding the tomb of one particular king, and that king Tutankhamun.'

As the opening of the tomb revealed, even Tutankhamun had not escaped some attention from grave-robbers. In the Antechamber and particularly the Annex someone had rifled through the pharaoh's appurtenances for the after-life 'about as thoroughly as an earthquake'. But this must have been very early on after Tutankhamun had been buried as very little was taken, and most importantly, the central, golden shrine with the pharaoh in his gold sarcophagus had been left untouched. So much was found in Tutankhamun's tomb that to this day no Egyptologist has managed to make a properly comprehensive evaluation. And since he was a comparatively minor pharaoh who died when he was only about eighteen, this tells its own story about what has been lost from the much larger but anciently looted tombs of powerful pharaohs such as Seti I and Ramesses II.

The major New Kingdom pharaohs and their known tomb locations

Date of death	Pharaoh	Tomb Location	
		18th Dynasty	
1492 BC	Tuthmosis I	Valley of the Kings	No. 38
1479	Tuthmosis II	Valley of the Kings	No. 42
1458	Hatshepsut	Valley of the Kings	No. 20
1425	Tuthmosis III	Valley of the Kings	No. 34
1401	Amenophis II	Valley of the Kings	No. 35
1391	Tuthmosis IV	Valley of the Kings	No. 43
1353	Amenophis III	Valley of the Kings	No. 22
1335	Akhenaten	Ravine near el-Amarna	
1333	Smenkhare'	Valley of the Kings	No. 55
1323	Tutankhamun	Valley of the Kings	No. 62
1319	Aya	Valley of the Kings	No. 23
1307	Haremhab	Valley of the Kings	No. 57
		19th Dynasty	
1306	Ramesses I	Valley of the Kings	No. 16
1290	Seti I	Valley of the Kings	No. 17
1224	Ramesses II	Valley of the Kings	No. 7
1214	Merneptah	Valley of the Kings	No. 8
1204	Seti II	Valley of the Kings	No. 15
1198	Siptah	Valley of the Kings	No. 47
1196	Twosre	Valley of the Kings	No. 14
		20th Dynasty	
1194	Sethnakhte	Valley of the Kings	No. 14 (?)
1163	Ramesses III	Valley of the Kings	No. 3
1156	Ramesses IV	Valley of the Kings	No. 2
1151	Ramesses V	Valley of the Kings	See Note A
1143	Ramesses VI	Valley of the Kings	No. 9
1136	Ramesses VII	Valley of the Kings	No. 1
1131	Ramesses VIII	Valley of the Kings	See Note B
1112	Ramesses IX	Valley of the Kings	No. 4
1100	Ramesses X	Valley of the Kings	No. 18
1070	Ramesses XI	Valley of the Kings	No. 6

Note A: Original tomb, No. 9, usurped by Ramesses VI. Final resting place probably undecorated, therefore unidentifiable
Note B: Not found. Probably went undecorated, and therefore unidentifiable

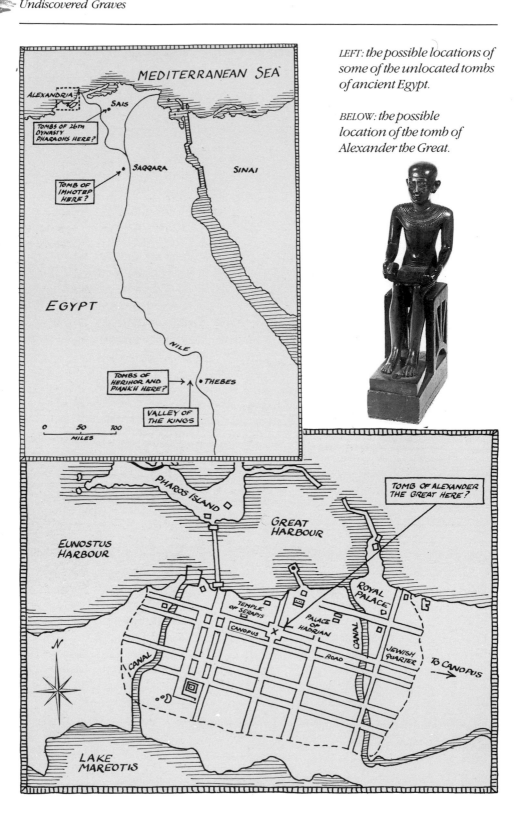

MEDITERRANEAN SEA

ALEXANDRIA

SAIS

TOMBS OF 26TH
DYNASTY
PHARAOHS HERE?

SAQQARA

SINAI

TOMB OF
IMHOTEP
HERE?

EGYPT

NILE

TOMBS OF
HERIHOR AND
PIANKH HERE?

THEBES

VALLEY OF
THE KINGS

0   50   100
MILES

LEFT: *the possible locations of some of the unlocated tombs of ancient Egypt.*

BELOW: *the possible location of the tomb of Alexander the Great.*

PHAROS ISLAND

GREAT
HARBOUR

TOMB OF ALEXANDER
THE GREAT HERE?

EUNOSTUS
HARBOUR

ROYAL
PALACE

TEMPLE
OF SERAPIS

CANOPUS

PALACE
OF
HADRIAN

CANAL

JEWISH
QUARTER

ROAD

TO CANOPUS

N

CANAL

LAKE
MAREOTIS

But even if no other Egyptian royal tomb comparable to that of Tutankhamun is likely ever to be discovered, what of the tombs of other of Egypt's great men, the viziers and the high priests? In common with their pharaoh masters, the majority of these have suffered similar depradations from grave-robbers, but could there be just the odd one that has been missed? As it happens, there are some important individuals whose tombs have never been located, and for whom no miscellaneous grave goods have turned up on the antiquities black market – crucial signs of possibly undisturbed graves lying somewhere, if only they could be found.

The earliest and most intriguing ancient Egyptian to whom this applies is undoubtedly Imhotep, Egypt's Leonardo da Vinci, the Third Dynasty genius to whom is accredited the design and construction of Egypt's oldest-known pyramid, the so-called Step Pyramid of pharaoh Netjerykhet Djoser (2630-2611 BC) at Saqqara to the south of Cairo. According to the late Egyptian historian Manetho, Imhotep was 'the inventor of the art of building with hewn stone', and his time and achievements were so generally regarded as a golden age that in the Graeco-Roman period he became deified as a patron of scribes, as a healer, a master sculptor, a sage and a magician. Yet Egyptologists are confident that he was a real-life flesh-and-blood individual. During the 1920s excavations at Saqqara brought to light an inscription with his name on the pedestal of a statue of the pharaoh Djoser unearthed near the entrance to the Step Pyramid. His name cropped up again nearby as a graffito on a stretch of the enclosure wall of the pyramid of Djoser's successor Sekhamkhet.

So what happened to Imhotep's own tomb? More than likely this would also have been at Saqqara, but the pioneering British Egyptologist Sir W. M. Flinders Petrie

FACING PAGE: Statuette of the sage Imhotep, accredited with the invention of pyramids, whose tomb Egyptologists hope to find at Saqqara.

RIGHT: Herihor and his queen Nodjme. Nodjme's tomb has been found, but not Herihor's. Could it still be intact?

The Valley of the Kings. Few hold out hopes of another unlooted grave such as that of Tutankhamun.

was consistently refused permission to excavate at this site, much to his frustration. In 1965 Petrie's quest was taken up with considerable enthusiasm by Professor W. B. Emery, who had succeeded to the Petrie professorial chair at University College, London, and then on Emery's death in 1971, by his successor Professor H. D. Smith. Although by 1976 these efforts had brought to light the mummies of some four million ibises, half a dozen hawks, and a score of sacred cows, they revealed no tomb of Imhotep. Nonetheless, the Saqqara site is by no means yet exhausted and can still produce some surprises, as is evident from the discovery there in 1950 of a complete Fifth Dynasty buried pyramid, unearthed by the Eyptian Egyptological specialist Zakaria Goneim. So, whether intact or, far more probably, long ago looted, the tomb of Imhotep may still be awaiting some future excavator.

Other important individuals whose tombs have not yet been found are the great Twentieth Dynasty officials, Herihor and his successor Pi'ankh who, at a time when the pharaonic Ramessid capital had been moved to the Nile delta far to the north, enjoyed near-pharaoh status at Thebes to the south. As has been noted by the Egyptologist John Romer, both Herihor and Pi'ankh had a particularly close relationship with the Theban professional tomb-makers at a time when these latter were specifically engaged in trying to restore order from the ravages of pharaonic tomb-looting that had occurred in earlier centuries. The mummy of Herihor's wife Nodjme has been found remarkably well-preserved due to an innovative technique of the Twentieth Dynasty period. But neither Herihor's nor Pi'ankh's tombs nor mummies, or anything from these, have come to light, strongly suggesting that these might have been so well-concealed that they are still somewhere, quite possibly undisturbed, far out in one of the uninhabited, waterless valleys of the hills to the west of Thebes. While any discovery would not be as rich as that of Tutankhamun, it could nonetheless be almost equally as interesting, and John Romer, in particular, hopes for some future success, subject to the granting of the appropriate excavation permits by the Egyptian authorities.

Internal strife, invasions and other factors sent Egypt's one-time magnificence into a marked decline after the Twentieth Dynasty, with even royal tombs becoming pale shadows of those of earlier, more prosperous times. Nonetheless, there were times of minor revival, such as during the Twenty-Sixth Dynasty, in the sixth century BC when the capital was at Sais in the Nile delta. Here, the Greek historian Herodotus, who visited the area, recorded viewing in a temple precinct the obviously not insubstantial tombs of King Apries (*c.*589-570 BC) and his usurper/ successor Amasis (570-526 BC):

> The people of Sais buried all the kings who came from the province inside this precinct – the tomb of Amasis, too, though further from the shrine than that of Apries and his ancestors, is in the temple court, a great cloistered building of stone, decorated with pillars in imitation of palm-trees, and other costly ornaments. Within the cloister is a chamber with double doors, and behind the door stands the sepulchre.

The site of Sais or ancient *Zau* is reliably known to be that of the present-day village of Sa el-Hagar, in the Nile delta on the right bank of the Nile's Rosetta branch, and up to a hundred years ago it was still possible to trace just to the north of the village the remains of a huge ancient mud-brick enclosure, a rectangle some 875 yards long by 766 yards wide, which may conceivably have been the precinct mentioned by Herodotus. Because of Egyptian peasants' time-honoured use of old mud-brick as a fertilizer, the structure has sadly almost completely disappeared, with the tombs and their contents no doubt rifled long ago. Nonetheless, because of the unpleasantness and difficulties of excavating in the mud of the Nile delta, to this day the site of ancient Sais has been relatively little explored, and might therefore yet offer some interesting surprises for the future investigator, although almost certainly much less spectacular than anything to be expected from Thebes.

In the unlikely event that anything of it has survived, by far the most interesting tomb in Egypt yet to be discovered is that of Alexander the Great, who conquered Egypt in the fourth century BC, and was undoubtedly buried at the Egyptian port of Alexandria. Here, after Alexander's unexpected demise in 323 BC, his former

A silver coin of Alexander the Great. His tomb was well-recorded in antiquity and at least the remains of it should lie somewhere beneath present-day Alexandria.

general Ptolemy built for the great hero a huge mausoleum, the Sema, at Alexandria's main cross-roads, where Alexander's body was enshrined in a magnificent gold sarcophagus. Subsequently, Ptolemy and his successors, up to and including the famous Cleopatra, all chose to site their tombs in the near vicinity. The Roman Octavian, later Emperor Augustus, on his take-over of Egypt from Antony and Cleopatra asked for and was granted a special viewing of Alexander's body, and gave this a golden diadem, some small compensation, perhaps, for an earlier, impecunious member of the Ptolemy dynasty having melted down the original gold sarcophagus and replaced it by one of glass. But by the beginning of the fifth century AD Alexander's tomb is no longer mentioned by visitors to Alexandria.

Despite this, the location of the original Sema with Alexander and his successors' tombs can still be reasonably confidently pin-pointed, being thought to have been in what is today south-eastern Alexandria, in the populous district commanded by the al-Nabi Danyal mosque. As recently as 1850 a Greek claimed to have seen Alexander's body beneath this edifice, and not long after an Egyptian said he had found in the near vicinity some ruins that may have been part of the original Ptolemaic tomb area, known as the Dema.

But since it would need wholesale demolition of a great many present-day dwellings to investigate properly this area, for the present anything of Alexander's tomb that might have survived is likely to remain undisturbed for some while yet. In the meantime, we have a not unworthy substitute. In 1977, at Vergina in Greece, Greek archaeologists unearthed a solid gold casket containing a partially cremated skull and other bones. They are virtually certain that they are the remains of Philip II of Macedon, Alexander the Great's father.

SOURCES:

HERODOTUS, *The Histories*, Book 2, trans. by Aubrey de Selincourt, London, Penguin, 1954, pp. 168-9

SUETONIUS, *The Twelve Caesars*, trans. Robert Graves, London, Penguin, 1957, pp. 59-60

BADIAN, E., 'Ancient Alexandria', *History Today*, Nov. 1960, pp. 779-787

BAINES, John, and Jaromir Málek, *Atlas of Ancient Egypt*, Oxford, Phaidon Press, and New York, Facts on File, 1980

CARTER, Howard, & A. C. Mace, *The Tomb of Tutankhamun,* 2 vols., New York, 1923 & 1927

EL-SAYED, R., *Documents relatifs à Saïs et ses divinités*, Cairo, 1975

RAY, J. D., 'The World of North Saqqara', *World Archaeology,* vol. 10, no. 2, London, Routledge & Kegan Paul, 1978

ROMER, John, *Ancient Lives, The Story of the Pharaohs' Tombmakers*, London, Weidenfeld & Nicolson, 1984

SETON-WILLIAMS, Veronica, & Peter Stocks, *Blue Guide, Egypt,* London, Ernest Benn, & New York, W. W. Norton, 1983

THE TOMB OF CHINA'S FIRST EMPEROR

No man can be said to have more dramatically changed the face of the earth than the Chinese emperor Qin Shi Huang Di, whose very name means First Sovereign Emperor of Qin, the territory we now know as China. It was Qin Shi Huang Di who in the course of his unification of what had previously been some half-dozen warring feudal states built the 3,700-mile long Great Wall of China, the one man-made structure said to be visible from the Moon.

Qin Shi Huang Di was only thirteen years old when, at that time simply known as Shi, he inherited the throne of his original kingdom, the semi-barbarous western territory of Qin, in 246 BC. Twenty-five years later, 'like a silkworm devouring a

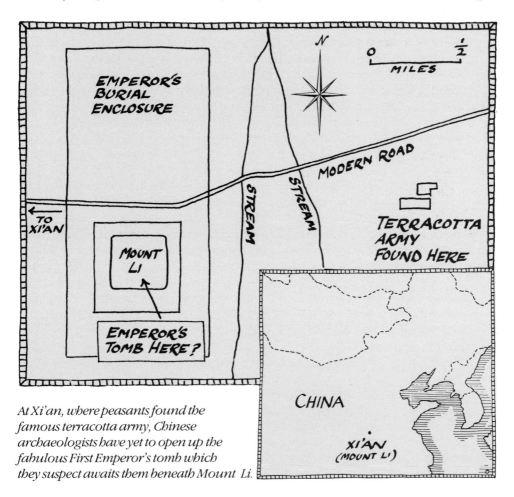

At Xi'an, where peasants found the famous terracotta army, Chinese archaeologists have yet to open up the fabulous First Emperor's tomb which they suspect awaits them beneath Mount Li.

mulberry leaf', as one Chinese historian was to put it, he was master of a vast domain stretching from the Pacific Ocean to the Gobi Desert, imposing upon all this a unified code of law, standardized weights and measures, a single written script, and, by no means least, the extraordinary wrapping of the Great Wall itself, to become labelled 'the longest cemetery on earth' from the vast numbers of conscript labourers who died in the course of its construction. As a direct precursor of the era of Chairman Mao, one of Qin Shi Huang Di's most characteristic, yet detested actions, was a 'burning of the books' – the destruction of most earlier works of scholarship, including all histories of states other than his native Qin. The very palace he built for himself typified the magnificence in which he lived – a mile and a half long and half a mile wide, with thousands of rooms. Yet Qin Shi Huang Di was so fearful of assassination that he generally chose to sleep overnight in one of his 270 lesser residences, each linked to others by networks of covered tunnels.

As might be expected, Qin Shi Huang Di was as concerned for the magnificence and security of his home in the afterlife as he was for that in the present, and almost his first action at the very start of his reign was to plan his own tomb, in which he is known to have been laid on his death at the age of forty-nine in 210 BC. Of the tomb there has survived an extraordinary description from the *Shih Chi (Historical Records)* of the Han Dynasty historian Si-ma Qian (145-*c*.90 BC):

> As soon as the First Emperor became king of Qin [in 246 BC], work was begun on his mausoleum at Mount Li. After he won the empire [in 221 BC] more than 700,000 conscripts from all parts of China laboured there. They dug through three underground streams; they poured molten copper for the outer coffin; and they filled the burial chamber with models of palaces, pavilions and official buildings, as well as fine utensils, precious stones and rarities. Artisans were ordered to fit automatic crossbows so that grave robbers would be slain. The waterways of the empire, the Yellow and Tang-tzu rivers, and even the great ocean itself, were represented by mercury and were made to flow mechanically. Above, the heavenly constellations were depicted, while below a representation of the earth. Lamps using whale oil were installed to burn for a long time.

As Si-ma Qian went on, Qin Shi Huang Di's successor decreed that his father should have for company in the tomb those of his wives who had not yet borne children. After these were duly buried:

> ... an official suggested that the artisans responsible for the mechanical devices knew too much about the contents of the tomb for safety. Therefore, once the First Emperor [i.e., Qin Shi Huang Di] was placed in the burial chamber and the treasures were sealed up, the middle and outer gates were shut to imprison all those who had worked on the tomb. No one came out. Trees and grass were then planted over the mausoleum to make it look like a hill.

That 'hill' was in fact a fifteen-storey-high, man-made mountain, which should have served to discourage even the most determined of looters. Nonetheless, according to Si-ma Qian, a few years later when after a series of insurrections Qin's successors were overthrown by what was to become the Han dynasty, soldiers did break into the tomb and desecrated it, along with looting and burning Qin Shi Huang Di's palace and destroying many of his monuments.

BELOW: The mound beneath which the tomb of the first Chinese emperor, Qin Shi Huang Di (RIGHT) is believed to lie. Some idea of the scale of what could be found may be gauged (FAR BELOW) from the tomb at Fengxiang of one of the First Emperor's Zhou dynasty predecessors, Duck Jing, which was opened in 1986 after ten years' work.

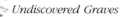

From that moment to this no one knows just how destructive the break-in to that tomb may have been. The memory of the site has never been lost, the original man-made mountain surviving to this day as a 165-foot-high, orchard-covered mound, some 4,600 feet in circumference, in the middle of a cornfield in the valley of the Huang He (Yellow River), forty miles from the ancient Chinese capital of Xi'an. In the environs of this mound, between 1932 and 1970 there were odd discoveries of buried life-size pottery figures which were interpreted as possible symbolic guardians to the original tomb.

One of the vast army of individually portrayed terracotta warriors which are still being unearthed at the approaches to Qin Shi Huang Di's tomb

But no one anticipated the scale of what might have survived until 1974, when a group of farm workers happened to be digging for a well a mile to the mound's east. They came across a series of life-size terracotta figures of men and horses apparently laid out in military order, and, as further test excavations were carried out by professional archaeologists, it became apparent that these were part of a vast army of similar terracotta figures, some 6,000 strong, covering an area of over three acres. Each figure was found to be individual, apparently modelled on a specific member of Qin Shi Huang Di's bodyguard. This whole army would appear to have been set up in a vast wooden-roofed pit until broken into, looted and burned, probably during the insurrections that marked the inception of the Han dynasty.

But despite the damage to some of the figures, (much of this from the collapse of the pit roof), and the fact that the looters took many of their accoutrements, nonetheless the extraordinary feature of the discovery is its vastness, and the extent to which so much has been preserved. So far, the Chinese archaeologists have been able to unearth only a fraction of the figures they know to exist beneath the soil, but already the site, over which a huge hangar has been built, ranks as one of the world's greatest archaeological tourist attractions. Besides the main pit, known as pit No. 1, test borings have already located three others, two with more figures like the first, and there may well be more yet to be discovered.

And all this raises the question: what of Qin Shi Huang Di's tomb itself? Preliminary investigation has revealed that in antiquity it had two protective walls, an inner one with four gates encompassing an area of 2,247 by 1,896 feet, and an outer one 7,129 by 3,196 feet. Within must lie the crucial central chamber? Even if only a fraction of its original treasures remain, the opening-up of that tomb is likely to be an event on a par with, if not surpassing, Howard Carter's now legendary unsealing of the tomb of Egypt's Tutankhamun. For the present the Chinese are in no hurry. They have many more years work bringing to light those of Qin Shi Huang Di's warriors known to be still buried in pit No. 1, and the central tomb site is scarcely one within the capabilities of the unauthorized treasure-hunter. But for the future, the tantalizing prospect could be one of the greatest archaeological discoveries of all time.

SOURCES:

SSU-MA CH'IEN [Si-ma Qian], *Shih Chi*, Chuang Hua Publishing Company edition, Shanghai, 1923

RAVEN, Susan, 'In China: The Find of the Decade', *Sunday Times Magazine*, 16 December 1979

The Smithsonian, November 1979

China Reconstructs, vol. 31, no. 2, February 1982

COTTERELL, Arthur, *The First Emperor of China*, London, Macmillan, and New York, Holt, Rinehart & Winston, 1981

THE TOMB OF ANTIOCHUS OF COMMAGENE

Some 250 miles south-east of the Turkish capital of Ankara, and high in the Anti-Taurus Anatolian mountain range, soars the 8,205-foot-high, cone-shaped Nemrud Dagh, or Mountain of Nimrod. As a location it is scarcely one of the most hospitable. Isolated and difficult to get to, in daytime temperatures can soar to 130 degrees Fahrenheit while the very same night they may drop to below freezing. There is neither shade nor water, and for thousands of years the main ascent of the mountain has demanded a gruelling four-hour journey, partly on muleback, and partly, by necessity, on foot, with a further three hours required for the return. The terrain is frequently lashed by wind, hail, torrential rain and blinding dust storms during which any attempt to travel is ill-advised.

Yet, here just over two thousand years ago Antiochus I of Commagene, a descendant of Alexander the Great, built a near 200-foot-high burial mound decorated by nearly thirty-foot high statues that even in their present-day state of ruin take the breath away. Antiochus of Commagene is scarcely a well-known household name, and even in the first century BC his kingdom was a comparatively insignificant one, important mainly as a buffer state between the Roman empire to the west and that of Parthia to the east, leading the Roman general Pompey to negotiate a long-lasting treaty with Antiochus in 64 BC.

But, as is clear from the monuments he left behind, Antiochus, who seems physically to have resembled Alexander the Great, set out to create more than a passing shadow of the latter's magnificence. Out of the Nemrud Dagh's living rock he had his craftsmen hew three great courts, or terraces, facing north, east and west, the two latter decorated by arrays of colossal statues, between twenty-five and twenty-nine foot tall, of himself and his personal pantheon of gods. Set as they are on twenty-foot high platforms, the statue arrays each have the scale of a five-storey building, and an inscription on the base of one of them makes clear Antiochus's motive for building so high on such an awkward site, precisely because this, the 'topmost ridge' of his kingdom, provided the 'closest proximity to the heavenly throne . . . of Zeus'.

Inevitably, with the passage of centuries most of the statues have been displaced and disfigured, with their heads scattered among the stone debris littering the site. Nonetheless, sufficient remains for archaeologists to have been able to deduce the general plan. On the East Terrace, facing a magnificent Persian-style fire altar, the statue array comprised in the centre Zeus, father of the gods, with the goddess of fertility at his right, a bearded Antiochus (who believed himself to be a god) at his left, and Apollo/Mithras and Herakles/Artagnes at either side. Such a fusion of Greek and Persian gods was quite typical for a principality at the crossroads between east and west, and on this terrace Antiochus decreed that into perpetuity there should be held monthly ceremonies with rituals and banquets all conducted by an impressive

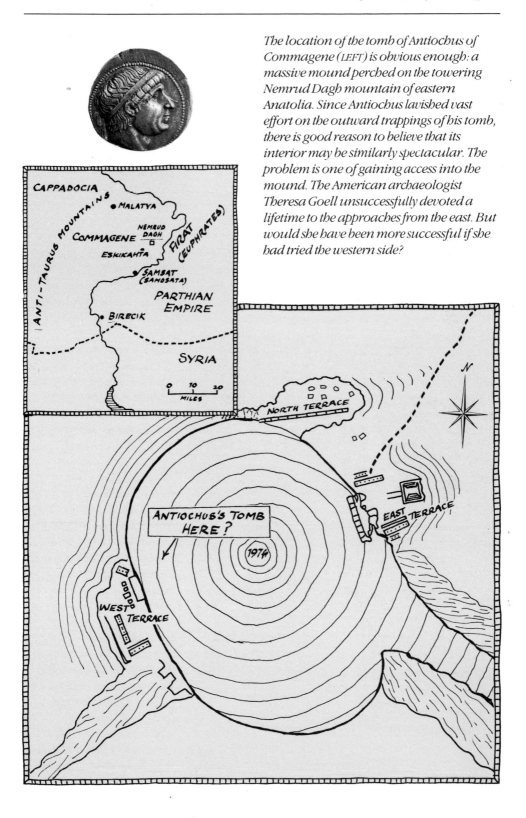

The location of the tomb of Antiochus of Commagene (LEFT) is obvious enough: a massive mound perched on the towering Nemrud Dagh mountain of eastern Anatolia. Since Antiochus lavished vast effort on the outward trappings of his tomb, there is good reason to believe that its interior may be similarly spectacular. The problem is one of gaining access into the mound. The American archaeologist Theresa Goell unsuccessfully devoted a lifetime to the approaches from the east. But would she have been more successful if she had tried the western side?

ABOVE: On what Antiochus of Commagene built quite literally as a throne of the gods, some of the twenty-nine-foot-high statues he commissioned for the West Terrace still stare out over the Anti-Taurus Mountains. Behind, looms the funeral mound inside which Antiochus's tomb may well lie intact.

LEFT: Among the West Terrace's dismembered heads lies this one of Antiochus himself, portrayed in youth with looks strikingly reminiscent of Alexander the Great, from whom he was descended on his mother's side. His father's Persian lineage is conveyed by the conical Persian headdress with its neckflaps for protection against the sun.

staff of priests and musicians. The other side of the mound, the West Terrace, Antiochus seems to have devoted to his Greek and Persian ancestors, including there another statue of himself as a beardless youth.

But the question to which the monument gives rise is, where might be the tomb which Antiochus, who died in 32 BC, arranged for his own remains? If the whole colossal enterprise was designed as his burial mound, his tomb, if unlooted and discoverable, should be one of no little magnificence.

The archaeologist who devoted much of her life to trying to answer this question was the Brooklyn-born Theresa Goell, who with her colleague, Dr Friedrich Doerner and various assistants conducted a series of excavations at Nemrud Dagh between 1953 and 1973. Theresa Goell's painstaking work, which has yet to be definitively published, revealed a great deal of information about the original appearance of the mound, including many inscriptions and sculptures and, from the remains of sculptured Greek horoscopes, the likely date of its foundation, 7 July, 61 or 62 BC. But up to the time of her death, at the age of eighty-four, in 1985, Theresa Goell and her helpers never managed to find the entrance to Antiochus's tomb. From her discovery of a rock core underlying the eastern base of the tumulus, she suspected this to have had its entrance from this direction, but every attempt to try and tunnel into this part of the mound became foiled by ominous avalanches of the small stones with which the monument was constructed. So to this day the mystery of Antiochus's whereabouts remains unresolved.

For any new venturer, one consideration that should be borne in mind is whether or not Theresa Goell was right to devote her energies so much to the eastern side of the mound. In the ancient world, rooted so much in worship of the sun, it was the west rather than the east that was associated with the dead, and usually it was from the west gate of any city that burial processions would depart. So was Antiochus buried on the western side? Whichever side, he seems to have arranged his burial with cunning as well as with magnificence, and until new engineering techniques are worked out his tomb, if it is indeed undisturbed, is likely to remain so for some while yet.

SOURCES:

GOELL, Theresa, 'Throne Above the Euphrates', *National Geographic*, vol. 119, no. 3, March 1961, pp. 390-405

Notice of Theresa Goell's death. *Biblical Archaeology Review*, vol. 12, no. 3, May/June 1986, p. 8

Fodor Guide to Turkey, London, Hodder and Stoughton, 1971

THE TOMB OF HEROD THE GREAT

If there is one act which the Jewish king Herod the Great is best known for in popular memory, it is the so-called 'Massacre of the Innocents'. As described in the opening chapters of the Gospel according to St Matthew, the 'wise men' who visited the infant Jesus decided for safety reasons not to tell Herod where they had found the child. Whereupon Herod, when he realized he had been foiled '. . . in Bethlehem and its surrounding district . . . had all the male children killed who were two years old or under.'

Herod the Great is a well-known, if scarcely well-loved figure from the generation immediately before the time of Jesus. When the Jewish Hasmonean (or Maccabean) king Mattathias Antigonus rebelled against Roman rule, Herod took the Roman side, and after a battle with the rebels, succeeded in reaching Rome, where he was nominated by Mark Antony as Rome's appointee as king of Judaea. It took until 37 BC before Herod actually managed to instal himself in the new role, but

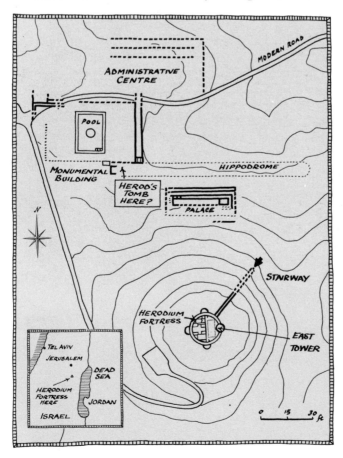

LEFT: The plan of Herod's retreat, Greater Herodium, as excavated by Professor Ehud Netzer. According to some opinions, Herod's tomb could be in the vicinity of the Monumental Building just south of the Great Pool.

FACING PAGE: Herod's alleged 'Massacre of the Innocents', from a painting in St Mark's Museum, Florence. Although not uncharacteristic of Herod, this atrocity is historically unattested other than in St Matthew's Gospel. If Herod was responsible Jesus must have been born before 4 BC, since Herod died in that year.

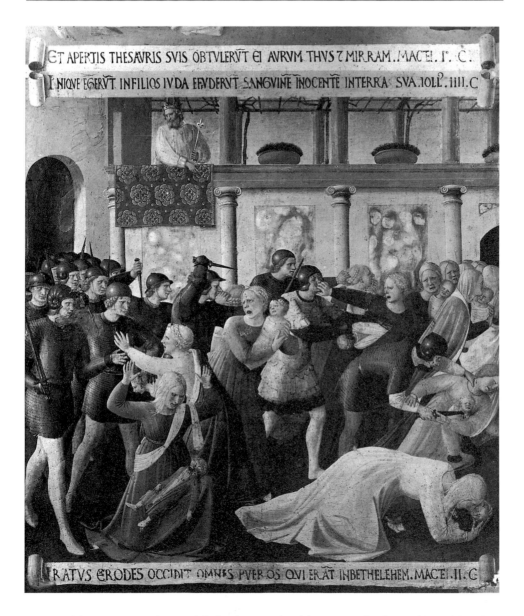

ET APERTIS THESAVRIS SVIS OBTVLERVT EI AVRVM THVS Z MIRRAM . MACEI. I'. C.

I NIQVE EGERVT INFILIOS IVDA ERVDERVT SANGVINE INOCENTE INTERRA SVA .IOLL? .IIII.C

RATVS ERODES OCCIDIT OMNES PVER OS QVI ERAT INBETHELEHEM .MACEI .II . C

once he had done so he established considerable power for himself, and lived in great magnificence. He reigned until 4 BC, and, while he was undeniably ruthless, murdering his own wife and two of his sons on suspicion of treachery, whether he was actually responsible for any massacre of young children such as that described by St Matthew is open to question. Certainly the Jewish historian Josephus, who left a full account of Herod's reign in *The Jewish War*, appears never to have heard of any such incident.

But Herod ensured that he left his mark on posterity in a variety of ways, not least in the well-constructed buildings he set up throughout his territories, his most ambitious, if ill-fated project being that of the magnificent Temple of Jerusalem,

An aerial view of Herodium fortress, originally equipped by Herod with every comfort, and designed to be near impregnable from attack

intended to be yet more splendid than that of Solomon. Begun in 19 BC, it was this work which Jesus's disciples are described as marvelling at in the Gospel according to St Mark Chapter 13:

> 'Look at the size of those stones, Master! Look at the size of those buildings.'

Such was the scale of the enterprise that some sixteen thousand craftsmen and labourers continued to work on the Temple's construction right up until AD 64. A further twenty thousand functionaries were employed, servicing it as a place of worship. Gold plates gleamed from the Temple's inner courts, and from its ramparts silver trumpets heralded the dawn each morning.

Among the other building projects which Herod initiated were construction of the port city of Caesarea, a new Samarian town called Sebaste (after Caesar Augustus), and various richly appointed palace fortresses, including the famous Masada excavated by the Israeli archaeologist Dr Yigael Yadin during the 1960s.

Inevitably, therefore, we would expect Herod to have made arrangements for himself to be buried in something of the same style and luxury in which he lived, and we are not disappointed. After a lurid account of the manner in which Herod died:

> . . . fever, an unbearable itching all over his body, constant pains in the lower bowel, swellings on the feet as in dropsy, inflammation of the abdomen, and mortification of the genitals, producing worms.

Josephus goes on to relate in similar detail the arrangements for Herod's funeral:
> Then they turned to the task of the king's burial. Everything possible was done by Archelaus to add to the magnificence: he brought out all the royal ornaments to be carried in procession in honour of the dead monarch. There was a solid gold bier, adorned with precious stones and draped with the richest purple. On it the body wrapped in crimson, with a diadem resting on the head and above that a golden crown, and the sceptre by the right hand. The bier was escorted by Herod's sons and the whole body of his kinsmen, followed by his Spearmen, the Thracian Company, and his Germans and Gauls, all in full battle order. The rest of the army led the way . . . followed by five hundred of the house slaves and freedmen carrying spices. The body was borne twenty-four miles to Herodium, where by the late king's command it was buried . . .

The location of Herodium, where Josephus describes Herod as having been buried, presents no historical difficulty. It is marked by a huge volcano-like cone, Jebel Fureidis, which dominates the Tekoa area some seven and a half miles south of Jerusalem, and is a site of very considerable archaeological interest. As established by archaeological excavations, here, within near-impregnable walls guarded by look-out towers at each of the four points of the compass, Herod built a private condominium, complete with gardens, an elaborate, Roman-style bath-house, and at the top of the eastern tower, a suite of rooms from which he could look out on the surrounding Judaean desert, Dead Sea and mountains of Moab.

Just to the north of this palace-fortress Herod constructed what would seem to have been the palace proper, one second in size only to Nero's later palace in Rome, with adjoining this a large hippodrome-type area, and a great pool, 210 feet long by 135 feet wide, the water for which had to be transported via a special aqueduct from springs three and a half miles distant.

Clearly, Herodium was a very special place for Herod. In fact it was at this particular site that he had won his crucial battle against Antigonus back in 40 BC, and it was the only location to which he seems to have given his own name. His decision to be buried there appears to have been a very deliberate and carefully take one, being notably in preference to internment in the mausoleum he constructed for other members of the family in Jerusalem.

This gives rise to the question, where exactly was Herod buried within the forty-five acres of Greater Herodium? Might his tomb still be there, perhaps undisturbed? One Israeli archaeologist for whom these questions have become something of a passion is Professor Ehud Netzer of the Hebrew University in Jerusalem, who has directed most of the excavations at Herodium in recent years, and has considered a variety of possibilities for the locations Herod might have chosen for his mortal remains.

For most scholars the favoured location has been somewhere within the massive eastern tower of the fortress proper, the construction of which was solid and significantly different from the rest, as if to hide a tomb. But Professor Netzer has disagreed, with very good reason:
> The ancient Jews did not bury their dead inside buildings, especially buildings that had been used as dwellings. They did not even use places attached to dwellings for burials. Tombs and cemeteries had to be isolated.

Accordingly, Netzer has focused his attention elsewhere, and in particular on a mysterious Monumental Building that appears to have once stood just to the south of the Great Pool. In one corner of this Netzer found some exceptionally fine pieces of Herodian masonry, with well-carved margins and elevated bosses.

In Netzer's description: 'Such elegant ashlars had appeared nowhere else at Herodium, not even on the mountaintop.' Disappointingly, careful investigation showed that these beautiful blocks of stone were no longer at the spot for which they were originally intended. They had been re-used sometime about the fifth century AD for the construction of a Byzantine church. The still-unanswered question, therefore, is whether these unusual stones might originally have been used for the entrance way to Herod's tomb, and if so, whether the original burial cave might still be discovered somewhere on the Greater Herodium site?

It is these questions, and the remote but conceivable possibility that Herod the Great's tomb might have been sufficiently well concealed to escape looting, that continue to haunt Professor Netzer. Herodium was taken over by Zealot resistance fighters when the Jews revolted against Rome between AD 66 and 70, and again during the Bar Kokhba revolt of AD 132-5. On the latter occasion a network of tunnels was built into the hillside to give the defenders extra hiding places. During these episodes or subsequently Herod's tomb could easily have been discovered and broken into, any valuables looted and the royal remains scattered to the four winds. But there is in fact no actual record of this ever having happened, and Herod, wily and resourceful individual that he was, might just have managed to elude those, ancient and modern, who would wish to disturb his rest.

Professor Netzer has still not lost hope of finding at least the original burial cave in which Herod was laid. He has a considerable amount of work to do excavating the Lower Palace, and welcomes serious helpers, among those who have assisted in recent seasons being the American New Testament studies professor, John McRay and a team from Wheaton College Graduate School, Wheaton, near Chicago. So, anyone who wants to find Herod's tomb would be best advised first getting to know Professor Ehud Netzer . . .

SOURCES:

JOSEPHUS, *The Jewish War*, 70, 670-673

GRANT, Michael, *Herod the Great*, London, Weidenfeld & Nicolson, 1971

NETZER, Ehud, 'Searching for Herod's Tomb: Somewhere in the desert-fortress at Herodium, Palestine's master builder was buried', *Biblical Archaeology Review*, 9, May/June 1983, pp. 31-51

THE GRAVE OF ATTILA THE HUN

During the early fifth century a name feared throughout Europe was that of Attila the Hun. Leader or *khan* of one of the heathen nomadic barbarian peoples whose movements westward had been responsible for accelerating the disintegration of the old Roman Empire, during a period of about twenty years Attila ruled central Europe practically from the Caspian Sea to the river Rhine. Early on in his career Attila behaved like a Mafia godfather, extorting lavish amounts of tribute or 'protection money' from the leaders of a Roman Empire already weakened by the Alaric incursion and its own internal divisions. He thus accumulated enormous wealth, and was able to live in considerable style.

Then in AD 451 Attila launched a massive invasion along the Danube to Gaul, meeting the combined armies of western Christendom on the *Campus Mauriacus*, the Catalaunian plains twelve miles west of Troyes. There were enormous losses on

Attila's men hid his grave so well that even the approximate location is conjectural: it is probably somewhere in north-eastern Hungary, beyond the river Tisza.

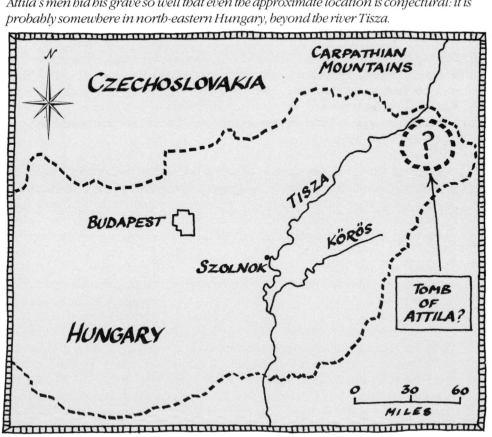

both sides, but effectively Attila was checked, and made a shrewd tactical retreat.

Undaunted, however, the following year Attila turned his attentions to Italy, blazing a terrible path of destroyed cities, Aquileia, Padua, Verona and Milan and others, in the course of a progress clearly directed towards Rome. The city of Venice is said to have been founded by those who fled before him. At the last moment, however, he stayed his hand from an all-out attack on the eternal city. He agreed to meet with Pope Leo I on the banks of the Po, and in the course of an extraordinary meeting between the two men, held at the height of summer, with Leo protected only by psalm-chanting monks, somehow Attila's mind seems to have been changed. It may have been the magnificent gifts which Leo showered on him. It may have been the Pope's solemn warning that an attack on Rome would be an attack on the Mother of God, with dire consequences for the future of Attila's immortal soul. Or perhaps it was simply that the Pope told Attila that the same armies that had checked him the previous year were gathering again. Attila broke camp that same night, allegedly promising 'I will leave the Mother of God in peace'.

Attila, in common with the rest of his people, was polygamous, and the following winter he took as yet another wife, a beautiful Germanic girl called Idlico. On this occasion the wedding festivities seem to have proved more of a match for him than all his previous military campaigns. The very same night, in a drunken stupor from all the alcohol he had consumed, he suffered a severe nosebleed. Choking on this, he died of suffocation, though not without, according to the pious Church chroniclers, calling upon Mary 'the great goddess of Rome' to spare him from the torments of hell.

When Attila's body was found, those who had fought with him mourned him in their traditional manner. In the words of a contemporary ambassador, Priscus:

> . . . as the custom of that race, they cut off part of their hair and disfigured their faces horribly with deep wounds so that the distinguished warrior might be bewailed, not with feminine lamentations and tears, but with manly blood.

Priscus describes Attila's burial:

> In the middle of a plain in a silk tent his body was laid out and solemnly displayed to inspire awe. The most select horsemen of the whole Hunnish race rode around him where he had been placed, in the fashion of the circus races, uttering his funeral song. . . . After he had been mourned with such lamentations they celebrated a 'Strava' as they call it, over his tomb with great revelry, coupling opposite extremes of feeling in turn among themselves. They expressed funereal grief mixed with joy and then *secretly* by night they buried the body in the ground. They bound his coffins the first with gold, the second with silver, and the third with the strength of iron, showing by such a device that these suited a most mighty king – iron, because with it he subdued nations, gold and silver because he received the honours of both empires. They added arms of enemies gained in battles, fittings costly in the gleam of their various precious stones and ornaments of every kind and sort whereby royal state is upheld. In order that human curiosity might be kept away from such great riches, they slaughtered those appointed to the task – a grim payment for their work – and so sudden death covered the buriers and the buried.

It is evident from this not only that Attila was buried with considerable riches,

riches the historical interest of which would far outweigh their intrinsic value, but also that, in common with the Chinese emperor Qin Shi Huang Di, the place of his burial was made such a secret that even the undertakers were killed so that the location might remain undetected. And so far as can be determined for more than

Attila the Hun, from a non-contemporary medallion portrait

fifteen hundred years, Attila's grave still lies somewhere, waiting to be discovered.

So where might it be? Among the difficulties is the fact that even the site of Attila's headquarters, which would at least determine the place from which the burial party set out, remains a matter of considerable historical conjecture. The ambassador Priscus who visited it, noted its simple wooden construction – which would inevitably leave little remains for posterity – and gave as the only clues to its location the information that he and his companions had to cross the rivers Drekon, Tigas and Tiphesas, wherever they might be. Most historians are agreed that Priscus and his party do not seem to have had to cross the major Hungarian river Tisza, or Theiss, and place Attila's headquarters as in the steppe somewhere north of Körös on this river, which would set it in the well-watered Szolnok region to the east of present-day Budapest. But according to some, 'Tigas' is probably a copyist's error for 'Tisas', which would mean that Priscus *did* have to cross the Tisza or Theiss.

Given such uncertainties, any organized search for Attila's grave is likely to have as much chance of success as the proverbial hunt for a needle in a haystack. For any Westerner, an additional difficulty is one of access. Short of some accidental discovery, therefore, the mortal remains of Attila the Hun, and any treasures that may accompany them, are likely to slumber on undisturbed for some long while yet . . .

SOURCES:

GORDON, C. D., *The Age of Attila, Fifth Century Byzantium and the Barbarians*, Ann Arbor, University of Michigan Press, 1960 (for quotations from Priscus and others)

THOMPSON, E. A., *A History of Attila and the Huns*, Oxford, Clarendon Press, 1948

THE GRAVE OF KING ARTHUR

One of the most colourful stories in English folklore is that of King Arthur, his Queen Guinevere, and the knights of the Round Table. It was the somewhat fanciful twelfth-century Benedictine monk Geoffrey of Monmouth who first gave full flesh to the story of Arthur in his *Historia Regum Britanniae (History of the Kings of Britain)*, Geoffrey claiming as his source a mysterious 'most ancient book in the British tongue', given to him by Walter, archdeacon of Oxford, a work that despite many efforts has never been traced.

Nonetheless, that there is some basis of truth to the Arthur story is evident from the sources earlier than Geoffrey of Monmouth that have come down to us, among these Nennius, the cleric in the household of the Bishop of Bangor, to whom we owe the first-known association of Arthur with the sixth-century Battle of Mount Badon (see page 41). The *Annales Cambriae*, or Welsh annals also provide some independent information on Arthur, including the battle in which he died:

539. The battle of Camlan in which Arthur and Medraut [Arthur's wicked nephew] were slain; and there was death in England and Ireland . . .

Glastonbury Abbey and the site of the alleged discovery of King Arthur's grave

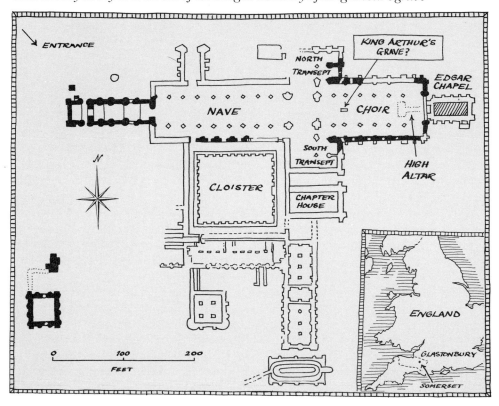

ABOVE: *The death of King Arthur, from a romantic nineteenth-century painting by James Archer*

FACING PAGE: *The ruins of Glastonbury Abbey as they look today*

In common with the rest of the confusion surrounding Arthur, ideas of where Camlan might be located have varied from north Wales, to Cornwall, and to Somerset. Certainly wherever it may have been, from there, according to Geoffrey of Monmouth, Arthur was carried to his last resting place, the Isle of Avalon. And from Avalon, Geoffrey hinted, Arthur might one day return.

While therefore Geoffrey seems to have obscured rather than thrown much light on the salient facts concerning Arthur's existence, nonetheless it was his work which effectively popularized the story of Arthur, particularly in the Norman court of Henry II, great-grandson of William the Conqueror. Henry was accordingly intrigued when, travelling through Wales, he was told by a bard of the exact location of Arthur's grave – purportedly a burial plot between two pillars or 'pyramids' to the south of the Old Church at Glastonbury in Somerset. Henry lost no time in telling

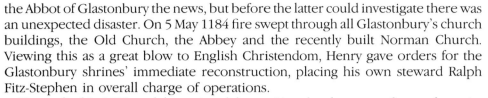

the Abbot of Glastonbury the news, but before the latter could investigate there was an unexpected disaster. On 5 May 1184 fire swept through all Glastonbury's church buildings, the Old Church, the Abbey and the recently built Norman Church. Viewing this as a great blow to English Christendom, Henry gave orders for the Glastonbury shrines' immediate reconstruction, placing his own steward Ralph Fitz-Stephen in overall charge of operations.

Henry died in 1189, and thus missed the exciting development of a year later. An Abbey monk who died requested to be buried between the two Old Church pillars that had been mentioned by the bard. This raised anew the question of whether Arthur might be buried at this spot, whereupon since any discovery of Arthur's remains promised to attract pilgrim finance for the restoration work, orders were given for excavation of the plot between the two pillars to proceed without further delay. The area was roped off, carefully curtained from prying eyes, and digging commenced.

The first discovery is said to have come when the diggers had reached seven feet down. Hitting a stone slab, they reputedly found on the underside a curious leaden cross with the inscription:

HIC IACET SEPULTUS INCLYTUS REX ARTURUS IN INSULA AVALLONIA
'Here lies buried the renowned king Arthur, in the Isle of Avalon'

Thus encouraged, the diggers returned to their task with fresh vigour, the monks joining in, whereupon at a depth of sixteen feet one of the shovels struck something large and solid and made of wood. As the earth was carefully scraped away, there emerged a hollowed oak log, stuck in the ground at a slight angle. A coffin? Crowbars and axes were vigorously applied, and soon bones began to be pulled from the interior, first a human shin bone which, as a monk demonstrated, was one of an individual who had been of no ordinary height, then a skull, smashed in by the left ear, as from a death-blow sustained in battle. Could this have been the very injury that Arthur was described as having received from the wicked Medraut?

Further bones followed, then from the end of the coffin some altogether more delicate bones which did not seem to belong to the same skeleton. Clinging to some of these were strands of yellow hair which crumbled away as a monk tried to pick them up. Too late, the name 'Guinevere' was purportedly spotted scratched onto the coffin. Had Arthur's famous wife been buried alongside her husband?

The immediate question that arises is whether any such coffin and bones were discovered back in 1190, or whether it was all a tall story put about by monks anxious for funds to help with Glastonbury's restoration work. This is all the more pertinent in view of the fact that the monks did not publicly exhibit the bones, but showed them only to a few select visitors. However, the Welsh chronicler Giraldus de Barri (more familiarly called Cambrensis) carried out his own personal investigation not long after the discovery had been made public. Although no fan of Geoffrey of Monmouth, he was nonetheless convinced.

Furthermore, as some hard evidence that it was not all fanciful, there undoubtedly was, from some source, the inscribed cross which the diggers allegedly found seven feet down. That this genuinely existed is evident from the fact that the antiquary John Leland reported viewing it at Glastonbury during the reign of Henry VIII. And William Camden, headmaster of Westminster School, provided a drawing of it in the sixth edition of his guidebook *Britannia*, published in 1607.

In itself however, this very cross does raise a certain element of the 'too good to be true' about the whole story. Why its specific mention of the location 'the Isle of Avalon', when anyone visiting the grave would inevitably have known where they were? And why the great disparity between the depth at which the cross was found, and that at which the coffin came to light?

There has been no uniformity of opinion among modern scholars who have examined the Camden engraving of the cross. In respect of the lettering, certain similarities have been noted with West Country crosses genuinely dating from the Dark Ages, and one authority, Professor Kenneth Jackson, has gone so far as to attribute it to the sixth century, the very period at which Arthur is thought to have lived. But Professor Jackson's view has not been shared by Professor Leslie Alcock of Glasgow University, and author of the book, *Arthur's Britain*. According to Professor Alcock: 'The inscription is not in the fifth or sixth century lettering, but several centuries later. In my mind, if the cross as illustrated ever existed, then it was a Tudor tourist trophy.'

As reproduced in William Camden's Britannia *of 1607, the controversial lead cross supposed to have been found by the twelfth-century monks on the site of the 'King Arthur' grave in Glastonbury Abbey. Scholarly opinion is divided over whether the lettering could genuinely derive from the Arthurian period.*

Such scholarly differences might be more easily resolvable if the actual cross was still in existence today. But it has been thought to have been lost without trace, unless any credence may be given to a strange claim of its re-discovery made in a letter received at the British Museum in November 1980. The sender of the letter was one Derek Mahoney of Enfield, north London, who had caused something of a stir in his local archaeological circles by the discovery of the place-name 'Camelot' on an old map of the Enfield area. Arguing that it was perhaps near Enfield that Arthur had held his court, Mahoney stirred sufficient local enthusiasm for a pond to be dredged in the hope of finding Arthurian remains. Although in the event the archaeological team found nothing, according to Mahoney, he re-sifted their dredgings, whereupon the Arthurian cross, of an identical size to that in Camden's engraving, came to light.

Mahoney was invited to take the cross to the British Museum, where it was examined by an assistant, Sue Young. But when she asked to be able to retain it for specialist tests Mahoney proved evasive, insisting on taking it back home. He became even more evasive when, after having openly claimed that the find had been made on Enfield Council property, he refused a court order to surrender the cross to the Council, who would legally be its rightful owners. Mahoney subsequently served a year's imprisonment for contempt of court, and the authenticity of the cross remains an open question to this day. It may be of some relevance that Mahoney happens to be an expert in moulding metal.

However, quite aside from the issue of the cross, there is at least some reasonable evidence that an exhumation of a genuinely ancient grave actually did take place at Glastonbury in 1190. The very fact that the 'Arthur' coffin was described as a hollowed-out tree trunk is of considerable significance, because this was certainly ancient Celtic practice, whereas the monks, if they had been faking Arthur's grave, might have been expected to provide for him a more fittingly regal sarcophagus of stone. And in 1962 a noted archaeologist, Ralegh Radford, who re-excavated the very same area of the Glastonbury ruins where the Arthur grave was said to have been found, came across unmistakeable indications of the ancient digging of a very large hole, which had subsequently been filled, complete with disarranged stones suggestive of the removal of an ancient grave. There is no mystery as to why Radford did not at this point come across the 'Arthur' and 'Guinevere' bones. Although the monks of 1190 reburied these, they were in fact dug up for a second time, in the presence of King Edward I in 1278. Reportedly, everything was exactly as had been described from the earlier excavations. Edward I arranged for them to be placed in a suitably prestigious black marble tomb before the high altar of the rebuilt Glastonbury Abbey, where they might have been there to this day but for the vandalism that accompanied Henry VIII's Dissolution of the Monasteries. Whoever the occupants of the 'Arthur' tomb might have been, this was rifled and its contents thoughtlessly tossed away.

So the mortal remains of Arthur and Guinevere could lie to this day in a sixteenth-century rubbish heap in some as yet unlocated portion of the Glastonbury Abbey grounds. Arthur's skeleton, at the least, might still be recognizable from his apparent exceptional height, and the great gash in his skull next to the left ear. Or the whole story of the discovery could have been a twelfth-century hoax. As yet, no one can be sure.

One alternative, somewhat off-beat possibility at least deserves mention. Very recently, in a new book *The Discovery of King Arthur*, the Arthurian expert Geoffrey Ashe, who lives in Glastonbury, has come up with a new interpretation of Geoffrey of Monmouth's puzzling mention of the 'most ancient book in the British tongue' from which he claimed to have derived his Arthur story. Since along with other authors who followed him Geoffrey consistently located some of Arthur's adventures in Gaul, i.e. France, might he have meant the Breton rather than the British language, and might Arthur therefore perhaps have lived – and died – in France rather than anywhere in Britain? Ashe found Continental authors of the fifth and sixth centuries referred to a king called Riothamus who apparently led an army of Bretons into France's Burgundy region, suffered betrayal at the hands of one of his deputies, then vanished after a terrible final battle without any record of his actual death. It all rather uncannily sounded like Arthur, the name 'Riothamus' raising no special problem, since it simply means 'Supreme King'. Ashe found himself inevitably wondering whether Arthur's Avalon might have been the French Burgundian town of that name, a few miles south-west of Auxerre.

If this is the case, then it would be at French Avallon, rather than at Glastonbury, that Arthur and Guinevere's remains should best be sought. And the battle of Mount Badon would similarly need to be relocated. But my personal option would be for keeping Arthur British . . .

SOURCES:

GEOFFREY OF MONMOUTH, *Historia Regum Britanniae*, translated into English in GILES, J. A., *Six Old English Chronicles*, 1878

NENNIUS, *Historia Britonum, c. 796*, translated into English in GILES (loc. cit., above)

ALCOCK, Professor Leslie, *Arthur's Britain: History and Archaeology AD 367-634,* London, Allen Lane, 1971

ASHE, Geoffrey, *King Arthur's Avalon, The Story of Glastonbury,* London, Collins, 1957

—, *The Discovery of King Arthur.* London, Debretts, 1986

CAMDEN, William, *Britannia*, sixth edition, 1607

RADFORD, Courtney A. Ralegh, *The Excavations at Glastonbury Abbey*, London, Pitkin Pictorials, 1966

SIMPSON, Colin, 'Double cross', *Sunday Times*, 3 April 1983

THE UNBURIED KING: JAMES IV, KING OF SCOTS

If there is an equivalent in Scottish history to England's King Arthur, that individual must be James IV, king of Scots, killed fighting the English at the battle of Flodden in 1513. Although James died a hero, the English never gave him a proper burial, so that to this day he has no known grave. And perhaps because of this mystery, during the centuries since his death the Scots have nursed a legend that James will one day come again.

However, the first significant difference between James and King Arthur is that James is a character altogether more firmly rooted in the pages of history. Contemporary portraits have been preserved of him, from which he stares out as a virile, clean-cut young man (although he subsequently sported a red beard), visibly shunning the ostentatious jewels and other royal trappings so favoured by his English counterpart, Henry VIII. The son of James III, who in 1488 was assassinated for favouritism during an uprising by his nobles, James IV was only a fifteen-year-old boy when he inherited the Scottish throne. Deeply shocked by the bloody manner of his accession, for which he felt a heavy burden of responsibility, he wore a penitential iron chain round his waist for the rest of his life, adding to the weight with further links each year.

Probably because of such a troubled beginning, James threw himself into the affairs of kingship with extraordinary vigour, earning new loyalty from his hitherto troublesome Gaelic-speaking northern subjects, improving general educational standards, encouraging the new Renaissance arts of printing and medicine, and building the *Great Michael*, Europe's largest and most impressive warship. He also tried to improve relations with England, heartbreakingly rejecting the Scottish love of his life in favour of a diplomatically more advantageous marriage with Margaret Tudor, daughter of England's Henry VII. But when Henry VIII, on ascending the English throne, began to behave aggressively towards James's long-term ally France, the old strains of Anglo-Scottish discord began to tell. The moment that he learned that Henry had landed an English army on French soil, James felt honour-bound to help out his old ally by invading England from the north, anticipating not unreasonably that with the real weight of English forces across the Channel, he would meet little resistance.

But although James was modern-minded in a variety of respects, he had seriously under-estimated both the efficiency of English defences and the technical innovations in weaponry and military tactics fostered under the Tudors. The man who stopped James's army near Flodden Edge, Northumberland early in September 1513, was a very astute old soldier, the Earl of Surrey. While Surrey, who suffered from gout, directed operations from the safety of a litter, James, following the old medieval ways, insisted not only on leading his army into battle, but also choosing to fight on foot. Remarkably, James actually succeeded in getting to within a spear's

King James IV of Scotland, killed at Flodden in 1513. Although one of Scotland's most enlightened kings, he has no known grave.

length of the Earl of Surrey's litter. But there he was cut down, together with his young son and many of the bravest and best among the Scottish nobility. According to a contemporary account of what happened to his body when this was subsequently found among the thousands of other Scottish dead on the battlefield:

> The king had divers deadly wounds and in especial one with an arrow, and another with a bill, as appeared when he was naked. After that the body of the king of Scots was found and brought to Berwick, the Earl [of Surrey] showed it to Sir William Scott, his [i.e. James IV's] Chancellor, and Sir John Forman, his

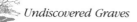
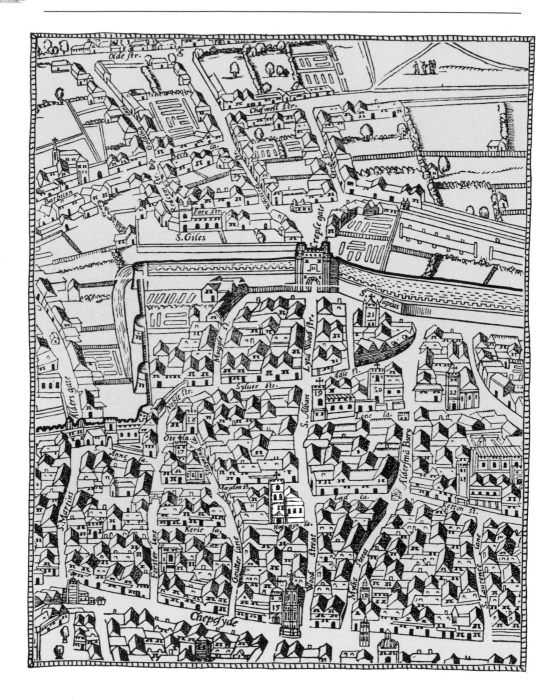

Part of a late sixteenth-century map of London, showing at the bottom Wood Street (off 'Chepesyde'), where James IV's head was kept for a while in the house of Elizabeth I's master glass-maker, Lancelot Young. According to the contemporary antiquary, John Stow, the head was subsequently moved to an unmarked burial-place in St Michael's Church (indicated) in the same street.

serjeant porter, who knew him at the first sight, and made great lamentation. Then was the body disembowelled, embalmed and cered [covered in wax, part of the embalming traditional for royalty at this period], and secretly amongst other stuff conveyed to Newcastle. . . . Then the Earl brought the body to Richmond.

At the English court at Richmond near London one person who viewed James's body with rather more pride than pity was Queen Catherine of Aragon, the first of Henry VIII's six wives. For her it provided tangible proof that she was able to take good care of England in Henry's absence. To show off her prowess, she immediately sent James's torn and blood-stained surcoat to Henry, who was still away in France. She even appears to have been minded to send James's corpse itself 'but our Englishmen's hearts would not suffer it'.

Because James happened to have died excommunicate, it was necessary for the Pope, Leo X, to send Henry a letter formally permitting the Scottish king's body to be given a proper burial in consecrated ground in St Paul's Cathedral (a building that would later be burned in the Great Fire of 1666). This Leo lost little time in doing, the letter being sent on 29 November 1513, little more than two months after James's death, a remarkable achievement for the communications of the time. However, almost immediately on arrival in England Henry became bed-ridden with an infection. Perhaps understandably, attending to James's burial appears to have fallen low on his list of priorities. But even when he had recovered by the following February Henry still continued to neglect his brother-in-law's burial, an omission which he never rectified.

As a result James's corpse, despite the care with which it had originally been embalmed, would seem to have been left for decades lying in the lumber room of a monastery at Shene in Surrey. There, according to John Stow, who wrote a *Survey of London* at the end of the sixteenth century:

I have been shown the same body so lapped in lead . . . thrown into a waste room amongst the old timber, lead and other rubble. Since which time workmen there, for their foolish pleasure, hewed off his head; and Launcelot Young, master glazier to Her Majesty [Elizabeth I], feeling a sweet savour to come from thence, and seeing the same dried from all moisture, and yet the form remaining with the hair of the head and beard red, brought it to London to his house in Wood St., where for a time he kept it for its sweetness, but in the end caused the sexton of that church to bury it among other bones taken out of their charnel.

Thus, according to Stow, James's head ended up disembodied, and 'without any outward monument' at St Michael's Church, Wood Street, off Cheapside in London.

But even this was not the end of the misfortunes of James's remains. For St Michael's Church, like the original St Paul's Cathedral, was gutted during the Great Fire, and although sufficient of the original structure remained for a temporary roof to be thrown over it, by an Act of Parliament, that of the Union of City Benefices, it was destroyed subsequently.

Wood Street itself has survived, still just off Cheapside, not far from where Sir Christopher Wren built the new St Paul's Cathedral. But now it is anyone's guess under which existing building might lie the foundations of St Michael's Church and with them, just conceivably, some ancient vault of bones with a bodiless head

RIGHT: A contemporary portrait of James IV, the Scottish king prophesied to 'come again'. Could his embalmed head even yet be found somewhere beneath the streets of London?

FACING PAGE: The now-demolished St Michael's Church, Wood Street, as it looked c.1890, more than two centuries after being gutted in the Great Fire of London

strangely better preserved than others of the period.

Even if it is among other human remains the partly mummified, red-bearded head of James IV is likely to be distinctively different. It should also be easy to check it against the king's several surviving portraits. So although admittedly a slim one, there is just the possibility that one day James's so ill-treated head might re-emerge, with it fulfilling the old Scottish legend that James IV, like England's king Arthur, really will come again . . .

SOURCES:

Manuscript, 'Hereafter ensue the trewe Encounter or Batayl lately don between Englande and Scotland . . .', Facsimile from Haslewood, 1809

Letter of Leo X to Henry VIII, Cotton, Vitell. B.2, 54

STOWE, John, *Survey of London*, 1598 & 1603

BELL, Walter George, *The Great Fire of London in 1666*, London, John Lane, 1920

SMITH, G. Gregory, *The Days of James IV*, London, David Nutt, 1900

SIR FRANCIS DRAKE'S LEAD COFFIN

As the man who, more than any other, was responsible for the repulse of the Spanish Armada of 1588, Sir Francis Drake has a well-deserved place in the uppermost ranks of England's heroes. Yet, while the hero of Trafalgar, Lord Nelson is buried with due honour in Westminster Abbey, one may look in vain for Sir Francis Drake's burial place anywhere in England – or elsewhere, for that matter.

For Drake died, and was buried, at sea. But not, as it happens, in the open sea. Both the circumstances and the location happen to be historically quite well attested. It was in 1595 that Drake together with his fellow seafarer Sir John Hawkins took an English fleet to the Caribbean on what was to be both men's last voyage. Not unusually for Drake, the expedition happened to be one which from the outset was

The approximate location, not far from the present-day Panama canal, where Sir Francis Drake's lead-protected coffin was buried at sea just off Portobelo.

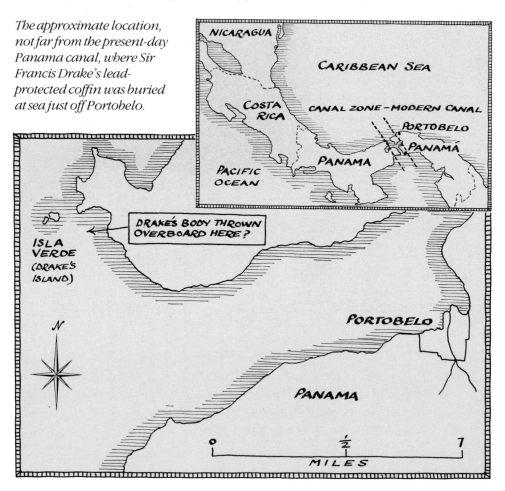

Sʳ **FRANCIS DRAKE** *one of the first of thoſe wᶜʰ in his Sea voyages put a Girdle about the World. He Died upon the Seas. Anno Dñi 1595 · W:M·ſculp:*

Sir Francis Drake, from an engraving of 1648, by W. Marshall. Could his body even yet be relocated and brought back to a hero's burial in England?

fraught with misadventure: quarrels between Hawkins and Drake, a thwarted attack on the Spanish town of Las Palmas in the Canaries, the loss to the Spanish of the *Francis*, a ship personally owned by Drake, the death of Hawkins just as a Spanish fleet was sighted off the island of Puerto Rico, and followed by the defeat of an English expeditionary force which Drake had sent on a land attack in the isthmus of Panama. By the time the remnants of this expedition returned to the waiting ships,

Drake's burial at sea, as romantically imagined by a nineteenth-century engraver. The gun salutes are certainly historically attested.

Drake himself was in the last throes of 'bludie flux', or amoebic dysentery. Shortly after, as the fleet attacked the Panamanian port of Portobelo, Drake breathed his last, being buried at sea the next day just outside the harbour of Portobelo in a lead-covered wooden coffin shot over the side of the royal galleon *Defiance*. In the words of an anonymous English observer:

> His corps being laid into a coffin of lead, he was let down into the sea, the trumpets in doleful manner echoing out this lamentation for so great a loss, and all the cannons in the fleet discharged according to the custom of all sea funeral obsequies.

That Drake's coffin was indeed covered in sheet lead appears to be confirmed from the expedition's surviving inventories, which show a discrepancy in the weight of sheet lead taken on the outward voyage, and that with which the expedition returned, of precisely the amount which would have been needed to cover a 6 x 2 x 2-foot wooden box. And since the *Mary Rose* discoveries have shown that human skeletal remains can survive hundreds of years' immersion in the sea if they become covered in sand or silt, theoretically Drake's body should be recoverable, particularly since the location of the burial spot is relatively well recorded. In 1601 the Plymouth privateer William Parker, who had been a friend of Drake, and subsequently became mayor of Plymouth, launched an attack on Portobelo, and in his reporting of this event in his Journal remarked:

> . . . Being safely come forth [from Portobelo] we rode in our pinnaces and shallops behind a small island which lay betwixt us and the Wester fort of St Iago, under my Vice Admiral Rawlins brought two ships thither, which rode somewhat to the Eastward of the Castle of San Felipe, under the rock where Sir Francis Drake his coffin was thrown overboard.'

Obviously, if Drake's remains could be found they would be of considerable historical and pathological interest. They might even merit a long overdue re-burial in Westminster Abbey. Such considerations were not lost on the marine archaeologist and writer Sydney Wignall who became interested in the search for Drake's remains during the 1970s. Closely scrutinizing William Parker's report, Wignall found an immediate anomaly: that whereas Parker stated that the Portobelo harbour entrance faces north, in fact it faces west. Clearly Parker must have had his compass bearing wrong at the time.

But far more importantly Wignall discovered in the Admiralty Library a slim, anonymously written volume grandiosely called *A Geographical Description of Coasts and Harbours and Sea Ports of the Spanish West Indies, Particularly of Porto Bello, Cartagena and the Island of Cuba.* This Wignall found to contain a most important Appendix: '. . . Captain Parker's own Account of his Taking of the Town of Port Bello, in the Year 1601, with an Index and a New and Correct Chart of the Whole,' As Wignall subsequently described this discovery:

> The tiny volume contained everything I could have wished for. There was a chart of the bay of Porto Bello, showing the forts and castles, and the town. The index contained all the references I had read in Parker's Journal, and under

Portobelo's Isla Verde or Drake's Island, a clue to where Drake's coffin went overboard?

A diver using an underwater metal-detector in the hunt for Drake's coffin during the marine archaeologist Sydney Wignall's unsuccessful expedition to Portobelo in 1975

Item C was the reference, 'The place where my shippes roade, being the Rocke where Sir Francis Drake his coffin was thrown overboard'. Parker's chart of Porto Bello showed item 'C' with small vessels anchored close to, and the rock 'C' was the Isla Verde of the American twentieth-century charts.

Wignall even found out how Parker would have learned where Drake's coffin had been laid to rest. A victualling officer called George Lawriman had been on both Drake's 1595/6 expedition and that of Parker in 1601, and must therefore have been able to point out to Parker exactly where he had seen Drake's coffin ceremonially tossed overboard. Wignall therefore not unreasonably judged that he had as near as possible a fix on where to find Drake's coffin, and could therefore justify the mounting of an expedition to try to locate this and bring it back to England.

In the summer of 1975 he arrived at Portobelo along with a team of divers and sonar equipment, and in the course of some six months work found an anomaly under the harbour mud which might have been Columbus's caravel *Vizcaina*, known to have been scuttled at Portobelo during his last voyage of discovery in 1503. Alternatively, it might have been Drake's ship *Elizabeth*, known to have met the same fate there shortly after Drake's death. Wignall also found a couple of wrecks of the seventeenth and eighteenth centuries. But although the discovery of a small lead block caused a momentary flurry of excitement (and accompanying press confusion), his searches failed to locate Drake's coffin. Wignall returned disappointed, but he remains convinced that the coffin is still there, and should be more readily detectable with the more advanced equipment available today. Since Wignall has, temporarily at least, lost his interest in renewing the search for Drake's body, the search remains open to anyone with the resources to mount an appropriate expedition to Panama.

Hopes to bring Drake back in triumph for a formal re-burial in Westminster Abbey might, however, be doomed for disappointment. Under Panamanian law any such discovered remains would be required to remain in Panama . . .

SOURCES:

ANONYMOUS, *A Geographical Description of Coasts and Harbours and Sea Ports of the Spanish West Indies, Particularly of Porto Bello, Cartegena and the Island of Cuba*

PURCHAS, Samuel, *Hakluytus Posthumus, or Purchas his Pilgrimes*, London, 1625 (for the quotation from William Parker's Journal)

WIGNALL, Sydney, *In Search of Spanish Treasure, A Diver's Story*, Newton Abbot, Devon, David & Charles, 1982

HENRY HUDSON AND
HIS COMPANIONS

Before the building of the Panama canal, one of the dreams of the early explorers of America was to find a route to China and India by way of North America, the so-called North-West passage. The hope was that if such a passage could be found, it might prove an easier route than via Cape Horn or the Cape of Good Hope.

One of the first English individuals to undertake such a quest was the adventurer Henry Hudson. In 1607-8 Hudson looked for the North-West passage while employed by the Muscovy Company, but was stopped by ice off the coast of Greenland. In 1609 his sponsors were the Dutch East India Company, and while working for them he managed to discover the Hudson river, on which stands the present-day city of New York. He sailed up the Hudson river as far as where Albany stands today.

At this stage Hudson's adventures were looking promising, as a result of which in April 1610 three financiers, Sir Thomas Smythe, Sir Dudley Digges, and John

Henry Hudson's name dominates any map of eastern Canada and he and his companions must lie somewhere among the region's chilly wastes.

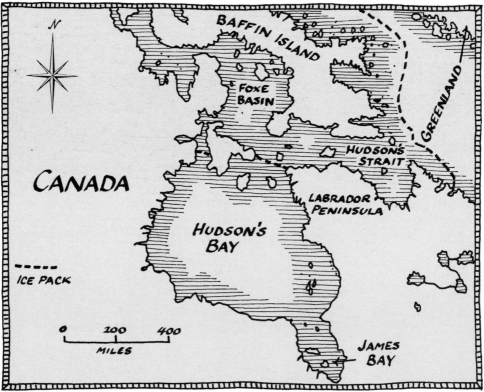

Cast adrift: Henry Hudson, his son and companions in the small, unprovisioned boat in which they were left to die.

Wolstenholme, provided him with a ship called the *Discovery*, and a crew of twenty-two, larger than he had ever commanded before, to continue the search for the North-West passage. On 11 May the expedition had reached Iceland, but even at an early stage Hudson was apparently having problems with his crew. Already by September he had found it necessary to demote two members, Robert Juet (or Ivett) of the Gun Room, together with the boatswain, Francis Clements, both of whom seem to have been fomenting mutiny.

By the end of October Hudson had succeeded in finding his way through the Strait named after him. He also discovered Canada's huge Hudson Bay and reached James Bay far to the south. But by this point the Canadian winter had already arrived.

Meeting conditions harsher than they had ever experienced before, the crew hauled the *Discovery* ashore and made themselves as comfortable as possible while they waited for the weather to improve.

Unfortunately, what Hudson had failed to anticipate was just how difficult it would be for a company of twenty-three men to find adequate food during such conditions. There was a great scarcity of game to be foraged, and so for long months the expedition endured conditions of near starvation, many inevitably becoming ill in the process. It was not until June 1611 that they were ready to leave where they had stayed over winter.

Shortly after they had set sail, however, having apparently headed into the ice of Hudson's Strait, the mutinous elements within the ship's company struck. At daybreak on the morning of Sunday, 23 June Hudson and his son John were seized, and together with seven other crew members, some of these sick, and one who of his own volition insisted on staying with Hudson, set adrift in the *Discovery*'s small boat, which had a sail, but no provisions of any kind.

Of the mutineers five were killed by the local natives when, a month later, they went ashore without weapons. Another was very severely injured during the same attack. Yet another, the mutinous Ivett, died during the voyage back across the Atlantic. The remaining seven, despite considerable hardships, managed to reach Ireland, and from there obtained help to get back to England. Having removed incriminating entries from the ship's log-book, they reported the circumstances of Hudson's fate to Sir Thomas Smythe and the naval authorities, effectively blaming the mutiny on the individuals who had subsequently died.

But the inevitable question is what happened to Henry Hudson, his son, and his other companions? The mystery of their fate, and the possibility that even after a considerable lapse of time they might somehow have managed to survive was one which caused a long delay in the surviving mutineers being brought to trial. It was only after six years that an indictment for murder was drawn up:

> Be it enquired for our Lord the King if Robert Billett . . . "mariner", Abacucke Pricket . . . "haberdasher", Edward Wilson . . . "barber-chirurgeon", Benett Mathew . . . "yeoman", Francis Clemence . . . "mariner", Adrian Motter . . . "mariner", Silvanus Bond . . . "cowper" and Nicholas Sims . . . "sailor" on 22 June, 9 Jas. in a certain ship of London called the *Discovery* of the port of London then upon the High Seas near to "Hudson's Straights" . . . with force and arms cruel hands upon John Hudson . . . mariner, master and governor of the *Discovery* did put and did "pinnion his armes", and put John Hudson his son, Arnold Ladley, John Kinge, Michael Butt, Thomas Woodhouse, Philip Staffe, Adam Moore and Sidrach Fanner in a certain "shallop" in the ice, did place without victuals, drink, fire and clothing, by reason of which they came to their death and miserably did perish . . .

Sims and Bond could not be found, but four of the rest suffered at least some term of imprisonment. Of Hudson and his companions there has never been any trace found. According to the barber-surgeon Edward Wilson, after they had been set adrift in the sloop they

> put out sail and followed after them that were in the ship the space of half an hour and when they saw the ship put one more sail and that they could not follow them, then they put in for the shore . . .

RIGHT: *The Franklin expedition grave amid the lonely ice of Beechey Island, in the North West Territories. Could the remains of Henry Hudson be similarly discovered one day?*

BELOW: *How northern Canada's permafrost preserves human remains. The body of Able Seaman John Hartnell, a member of the ill-fated Franklin expedition of 1845*

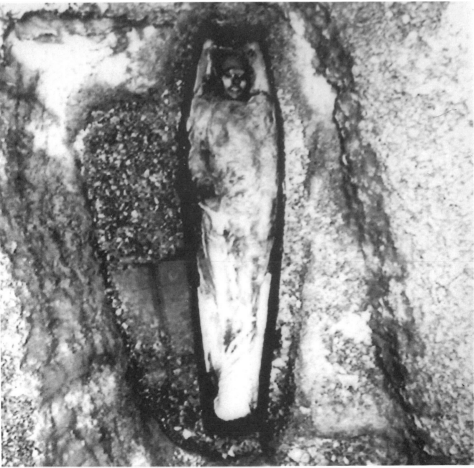

From this and from the information that even in June there was ice in the territory in which Hudson and his companions were set adrift, two deductions can be made. First, that Hudson and his companions are likely to have perished on land, rather than in the sea. Second, that since the territory was clearly an extremely icy one far to the north, presumably in the part of Canada known as the North West Territories, their bodies are likely to have been preserved and may, even after the lapse of nearly four centuries, be re-discovered.

That such a possibility is not a mere pipe-dream has been reinforced recently by the unearthing by a Canadian anthropological expedition of the bodies of two members of a later and similarly ill-fated attempt to discover the North-West passage, that of the nineteenth-century English rear-admiral and Arctic explorer, Sir John Franklin. Franklin, like Hudson, made three attempts to discover the North-West passage, his third being with two ships, the *Erebus* and *Terror*, which set out from Greenhithe on 19 May 1845, and were last seen on 26 July of the same year.

After expeditions were sent out in search of Franklin, bodies were eventually found, among these those of twenty-year-old Petty Officer John Torrington and twenty-five-year-old Able Seaman John Hartnell who it was established had died in 1846. They were given a proper burial amid the ice, and these were the bodies which the Canadian anthropological team, under the direction of Professor Owen Beattie of Alberta University, exhumed in 1984, finding them almost perfectly preserved by the permafrost in which they had been laid. As remarked by Professor Beattie, even after 138 years they looked more alive than dead: 'It is like a time-machine, seeing someone who looks as they did 138 years ago, wearing their clothing.'

The interesting possibility, therefore, is that one day Henry Hudson and his companions might be found similarly well-preserved, the time-machine effect being stretched to four centuries. The problem for any specific search is the vastness, emptiness and inhospitable climate of Canada's North West Territories. But the chance of an accidental discovery is always there . . .

SOURCES:

ASHER, G. M., *Henry Hudson the Navigator*, Hakluyt Society, 1860

L'ESTRANGE EWEN, C., *The North-West Passage*, privately published pamphlet, 1938

'Fate of doomed Arctic explorer', article in *The Times*, Friday, 28 September 1984

PURCHAS, Samuel, *Purchas His Pilgrimes*, Glasgow ed., 1906, vol. 13, pp. 377-410

EVEREST CLIMBERS,
MALLORY AND IRVINE

Before the successful conquest of Mount Everest by Sir Edmund Hillary and his Sherpa guide, Tenzing Norgay, announced the very day of the Coronation of Queen Elizabeth II, the British expedition which came closest to success was that of Lieutenant-Colonel E. F. Norton in 1924. While Norton himself may not be well remembered, the names of two of his team, George Leigh Mallory and Andrew Comyn Irvine, rank among the most illustrious in the annals of mountaineering. For, in fact, Mallory and Irvine may well have beaten Hillary and Tenzing to the summit by nearly three decades, the mystery arising because the pair, who certainly came close to success, never returned, and so far their bodies have never been found.

Of the two, George Mallory, a thirty-seven-year-old Liverpool schoolmaster and decorated survivor of the carnage of the First World War, was altogether the more experienced, having taken part in two previous Everest expeditions. By contrast Andrew 'Sandy' Irvine was only twenty-two years old, and was tackling Everest for the first time. But Irvine, tall and broad-built, was superbly fit – he had rowed for Oxford the two years previously – and had amply demonstrated his climbing skills

The approach to the summit of Mount Everest is the setting for the continuing mystery surrounding the deaths of the pioneer mountaineers, Mallory and Irvine. On 8 June 1924 they set off from Camp VI, never to return. Their bodies have never been found.

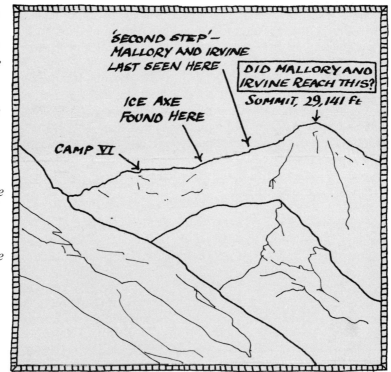

LEFT: Mount Everest looking towards the summit as photographed by Odell. Did Mallory and Irvine reach the summit before they were killed?

FACING PAGE: twenty-two-year-old Sandy Irvine, who had a flair for handling the expedition's technical equipment, which included innovative oxygen-breathing apparatus

in the Alps and Spitzbergen. Furthermore, he had a natural ingenuity with technical gadgetry. Besides having worked on an early form of automatic pilot for aircraft he sorted out problems with the expedition's pressure stoves, and proved exceptionally proficient with the venture's at-that-time novel use of oxygen equipment to help breathing at high altitudes.

Even before the final assault in which the two men lost their lives, the expedition had faced some severe difficulties. In mid-May 1924, while still in the process of establishing the chain of camps from which the summit could be attempted, they had been 'discomfited, but very far from defeated' by appalling weather. There followed a twenty-six-hour blizzard, and five nights of temperatures 50 degrees Fahrenheit below freezing point. Due to a serious loss of morale in such conditions, four of the expedition's porters needed rescuing from the highest camp achieved, Camp IV on the North Col.

Mallory, who was one of the three to rescue the porters, only seemed to be spurred on to greater effort by such difficulties – although he was realistic about the dangers. As he wrote in what would be one of his last dispatches,

> Action is only suspended before the more intense action of the climax. The issue will be decided shortly. The third time we walk up East Rongbuk Glacier will be the last, for better or worse. . . . We expect no mercy from Everest.

By early June the expedition had managed to set up six camps, a Camp V at 25,000 feet, and a Camp VI at 27,000 feet, established by team members Norton and Somervell in a record-breaking climb on 3 June. All was ready for a determined final assault on the 29,000-foot summit, and on 6 June, after a breakfast of fried sardines, Mallory and Irvine left Camp III with five porters to make their way steadily upwards to Camp VI, while the expedition's geologist, Noel Odell, with two porters, success-fully achieved Camp V. On 8 June, with the weather as not unfavourable of intermittent cloud and light snowfalls Odell worked on a geological survey of the mountain face between Camps V and VI, while Mallory and Irvine set out from Camp VI with one undoubted aim – to reach the peak that day.

As Odell, today a ninety-six-year-old Cambridge professor, recorded in a dispatch published in *The Times* in 1986:

> At 12.50, just after I had emerged in a state of jubilation at finding the first definite fossils on Everest, there was a sudden clearing of the atmosphere, and the entire summit, ridge, and final peak of Everest were unveiled. My eyes became fixed on one tiny black spot silhouetted on a small snowcrest behind a rock-step in the ridge, and the black spot moved. Another black spot became apparent and moved up the snow to join the other on the crest. The first then approached the great rock-step and shortly emerged at the top; the second did likewise. Then the whole fascinating vision vanished, enveloped in cloud once more.

> There was but one explanation. It was Mallory and his companion moving, as I could see even at that great distance, with considerable alacrity, realizing doubtless that they had none too many hours of daylight to reach the summit from their present position and return to Camp VI at nightfall. The place on the ridge mentioned is a prominent rockstep at a very short distance from the base of the final pyramid, and it was remarkable that they were so late in

High on the slopes of Mount Everest, the last-known photograph of Mallory and Irvine, prior to their disappearance

reaching this place. According to Mallory's schedule, they should have reached it several hours earlier if they had started from the high camp as anticipated. That they had encountered bad conditions and snow-covered rocks and other obstacles was likely. However, in my opinion, from the position in which they were last seen, they should have reached the summit at 4pm at latest, unless some unforeseen and particularly difficult obstacle presented itself on the final pyramid. This seemed to be very unlikely, for we had scrutinized the last slopes with telescopes and binoculars and had seen that technically the climbing was easy. Perhaps the two most likely explanations of their failure to return were a fall or inability to reach camp before darkness set in. I rather incline to the latter view and consider it very probable that they sheltered in some rock recess and fell asleep, and a painless death followed, due to the excessive cold at those altitudes. . . . Considering all the circumstances and the position they had reached on the mountain, I personally am of opinion that Mallory and Irvine must have reached the summit.

Heroically, at a height of 27,500 feet and without the support of any oxygen, Odell searched for two hours for signs of Mallory and Irvine's bodies, without success. On 19 June the expedition leader Lieutenant-Colonel Norton was obliged to cable back to England: Mallory and Irvine killed on last attempt. Rest of party arrived at base camp all well.

Of the all-too-meagre clues to their fate that have so far come to light one has been an ice axe found by the Everest adventurers Wyn Harris and Wager in 1933 at a height of about 27,600 feet, sixty feet below the North-east Ridge. Made by Willisch of Täsch in the Swiss Valois, this axe was thought to have belonged to one of the two missing climbers, although recently this has been doubted.

Apart from this, in 1979 a Chinese mountaineer reported having seen the body of an Englishman in tattered clothing lying some 2,000 feet below the summit. Unfortunately this informant died before his story could be properly verified, but the report acted as a spur to an American adventurer, Tom Holzel of Concord, New Hampshire, who in 1986 was mounting a three-month expedition to Everest with the aim of finding not only the bodies of Mallory and Irvine, but also their cameras. Not only would the bodies most likely be well preserved at such high altitudes, it is quite likely that with special processing the film in the cameras might be capable of being developed and thus determine for once and for all whether Hillary and Tenzing really were the first men to stand on the Everest's peak, or whether the gallant Mallory and Irvine preceded them.

Inevitably, such an expedition is not without its critics. The British mountaineer Jim Perrin, has written in the magazine *High* that Holzel's expedition '. . . disgusts me – and this is an entirely personal opinion – as nothing else in mountaineering history . . . ever has done.'

Somewhat less forthrightly, Sir Edmund Hillary, now New Zealand's High Commissioner to India, commented in a lecture to the Explorers' Club of New York: 'I would have thought Mallory had the right to be left sleeping in peace on his mountain.' This is a view shared by Irvine's surviving brother, A. S. Irvine. But the Irvine family is by no means unanimous on the issue, as is clear from a letter by Irvine's nephew, William Summers, published in *The Times* on 7 July 1986:

> I am sure Sandy, with his inquiring mind, would be happy that there is still interest and speculation over their achievement, and would not think of the proposed search as desecration. The finding of a camera with viable films, or even evidence from position of remains, might finally close the saga one way or the other. I wish the Americans every success.

Will Mallory and Irvine's remains be discovered? Such has become human mastery of the highest peaks and deepest ocean depths that there seems the strongest likelihood that someone, sometime will indeed find them, perhaps even before this book has reached publication . . .

SOURCES:

News reports in *The Times*, 21 June and 5 July 1924

Associated Press report 'US team tackles Everest mystery' in *The Times*, 1 July 1986

Letters to *The Times*, 7 and 10 July 1986

Correspondence with William Summers, Irvine's nephew and A. S. Irvine, Irvine's brother

CARR, Herbert (ed.), *The Irvine Diaries*, Gastons-West Col Publications

NEWBY, Eric, *Great Ascents*, Newton Abbot, Devon, David & Charles, 1977

Part III
Undiscovered Wrecks

*In the world of the undiscovered, undoubtedly the most
flourishing aspect in the 1980s is that of underwater
exploration, which has come a long way since the
primitive methods of the eighteenth century. Improved
sub-aqua equipment, robot submarines, underwater
television, underwater metal-detectors, and not least, the
development of special sonar for detecting solid objects
beneath sea-bed silt, have all combined to ease accessibility
to the world's many thousands of sunken wrecks, ancient
and modern. Inevitably, it is a field which has attracted its
own particularly vigorous element of treasure-hunters,
their sights firmly set on those ships known to have gone
down laden with cargoes of silver and gold. But there are
also lost ships which may not necessarily have precious
contents, but which could be of priceless historical interest
if rediscovered. These are just some of them . . .*

THE GREEK STATUES WRECK

Just how well Greek bronze statues can survive millenia of immersion in sea water is well demonstrated by a larger than life-size, fifth-century BC statue of a bearded male god daily admired by the thousands of visitors to Athens National Archaeological Museum. The god has his arms at full stretch, one behind and one in front of him in an action that suggests him having been about to throw a trident or a thunderbolt. Unfortunately, whichever of these two the object was, it is now lost, a somewhat frustrating fact as scholars identify the god as either Poseidon or Zeus depending upon which weapon they believe him to have held, and only discovery of the original would resolve the matter. Although this may seem a mere academic nicety, it raises the question of where the statue was found, and whether the original weapon, and any interesting accompanying objects, might still be recoverable.

Cape Artemision is the setting for the wreck of a vessel carrying priceless ancient Greek statuary.

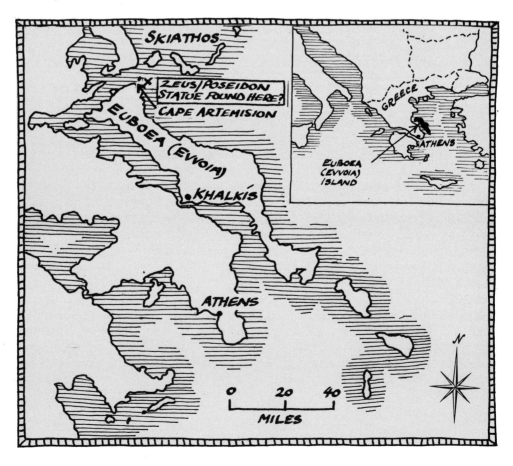

The god fished from the sea. But is he Poseidon or Zeus? Much depends on whether he carried a trident or a thunderbolt.

The discovery of the statue was, in fact, made in chance circumstances in 1927. Abutting the Greek mainland a little to the north-east of Athens lies the large and mostly unspoilt island of Euboea, the northernmost point of which is Cape Artemision, historically the setting for an opening naval skirmish between the fleets of the Greeks and the Persians in 480 BC. In 1927 some fishermen were hauling in their nets just off this cape when they felt a resistance, as if the net was snagged at the bottom. When a sponge-diver was sent to investigate, the cause was found to be the net caught on what looked like an arm sticking up from the sea-bottom, some 140 feet below. This was wrenched away and brought to the surface whereupon it was seen to be made of bronze, apparently having come from some ancient statue that was presumably still buried on the sea-bed.

Interested in whether his find might be of some value, the sponge-diver took the arm to the German Archaeological Institute in Athens, where it was examined by a Professor George Karo. Immediately recognizing the object's importance – although there were originally hundreds of bronzes made during the heyday of classical Greek art, most were melted down during the Middle Ages – Karo did some careful bargaining. Correctly anticipating that the arm came from a statue that

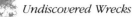

The lively jockey boy from the Greek statues wreck. Parts of his bronze horse were also recovered. But what else still remains beneath the sea?

was part of the cargo of an ancient shipwreck, Karo gained the diver's agreement to point out the exact location of the find, and then organized an expedition to the site, funded by the wealthy Greek cotton merchant, Alexander Benaki.

It was a time before the modern developments in underwater exploration, and the divers sent down were simple sponge divers who found that whatever the original wreck may have been, it was deeply buried in the mud of the sea floor. Although, at 140 feet down, they were working at well below their normal depths they managed to retrieve the body belonging to the arm, which turned out to be the Zeus/Poseidon statue. And they also brought to the surface a superb third century BC bronze of a lively jockey boy, together with a substantial number of bits from his horse, today also restored and brilliantly reconstructed in the Athens National Archaeological Museum.

But suddenly there was tragedy. As is well known, it is important for underwater divers not to return too quickly to the surface because of the problems which can arise from decompression. For some unknown reason one of the Benaki expedition's divers ignored all the safety rules, shot to the surface, clambered laughing onto the support vessel, then immediately dropped dead from the resulting embolism. The expedition was promptly abandoned, and all knowledge of the wreck's location subsequently lost. Although two years later the classical archaeologist, Dr George Milonas tried to rediscover the site of the wreck using divers equipped with professional 'hard-hat' helmeted diving suits, this was unsuccessful. .

In Athens the arm of the Zeus/Poseidon statue was skilfully re-attached to the recovered body, and the whole immersed in a huge tank of distilled water in order to absorb impurities from the bronze. The British classics specialist, Dr Charles Seltman, who viewed it at the time, described it as 'the most perfect bronze athlete statue that has survived from antiquity'. But the fact that its date is unquestionably fifth century BC and its companion jockey boy is third century BC strongly suggests that the ship which originally carried them was most likely not from either period, but from sometime later, the statues at that time already being antiques. This might have been during the Roman era, or, if in view of the place of discovery the ship's destination was Constantinople, sometime after the fourth century AD, when the city was capital of the eastern Roman Empire.

Either way, the wreck is likely to have been carrying substantially more high quality classical works of art than those found by the sponge divers, and if it could be located the world's all-too-scanty collection of Greek sculptures might be considerably enriched. Given present-day sonar techniques and other advanced underwater archaeological methods, plus the clue that the wreck was 140 feet down off Cape Artemision, the task of relocating the wreck site should not be too difficult, nor too unpleasant, as the waters off Greece are both clear and relatively warm. And if a bronze thunderbolt or trident happens to be found lying amid the debris, scholars might even be able to resolve their differences over whether the Athens Museum statue represents Zeus or Poseidon.

So the quest for the Artemision wreck is both a feasible and attractive one, although strictly for the professionals. As in Italy the Greek government rightly lays claim to all antiquities found on its soil and in its territorial waters. And ancient Greek statuary is so rare, and so well known among the world museum fraternity, that any new items turning up in salerooms would automatically cause the most intensive inquiries into the provenance.

SOURCES:

Regrettably there appears to be no truly authoritative contemporary account of the Cape Artemision wreck discovery, only a variety of semi-anecdotal stories, hence the mystery of the exact location. The secondary sources used here were:

BASCOM, Willard, *Deep Water, Ancient Ships*, Newton Abbot, Devon, David & Charles, 1976

CLEATOR, P. E., *Underwater Archaeology*, London, Robert Hale, 1973

SELTMAN, Charles, *The Twelve Olympians*, London, Pan Books, 1952

THE LOST WHITE SHIP

In 1120 England had been ruled for some fourteen years by the Norman king Henry I, son of William the Conqueror. With kingdoms on both sides of the English Channel, Henry inevitably divided his time between the two, and in the autumn of 1120 had concluded a particularly productive phase in Normandy, during which time he had increased his power and international standing at the expense of Louis VI, king of France. After an almost bloodless skirmish and diplomatic coup, Louis found himself obliged to recognize Henry I's son William the Atheling as heir to Normandy, in place of his own candidate, William the Clito.

By 25 November Henry was ready to return to England from Normandy, sailing from Barfleur, the very port from which his father William had set out to make his historic conquest in 1066. Just before he was about to leave a ship's captain came up to him, telling him that his father had been captain of one of William's victorious ships, and he in his turn would be very honoured if Henry would travel in his own, brand-new *White Ship* which was waiting at the quayside. Henry declined, as his own ship was already fitted out. But so as not to offend the captain, he agreed that

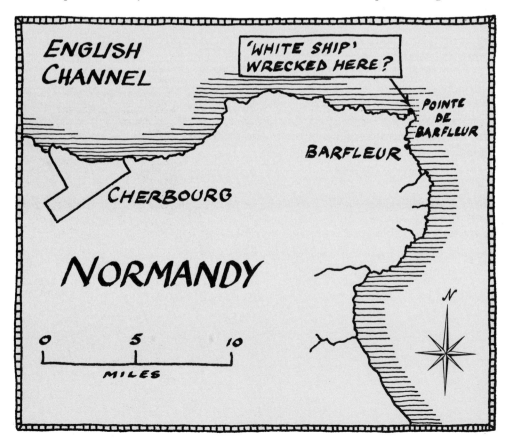

ABOVE: *King Henry I of England mourning the death of his son, from a contemporary manuscript. News of the disaster rocked the nobility on both sides of the English Channel, just as the sinking of the* Titanic *shook the wealthy of Britain and the USA eight centuries later.*

RIGHT: *The* White Ship *in which William the Atheling and his retinue were lost, from a contemporary manuscript. Location of the wreck could reveal fascinating insights of court life of the early twelfth century.*

FACING PAGE: *the Pointe de Barfleur in Normandy is where the* White Ship *was wrecked in 1120.*

The Pointe de Barfleur, as it appears today. Beneath its fast-flowing waters at least something must remain of the White Ship. *But the currents here are swift and treacherous for underwater exploration.*

the *White Ship* should carry his son William the Atheling, together with William's young courtiers, and all their accompanying riches.

At the time Henry's ship made its departure, William and his companions were still feasting in Barfleur, and in order that the crew of the *White Ship* should not feel left out of the festivities, casks of wine were sent on board. It was to prove a fatal act of generosity. When the ship eventually slipped out of Barfleur that evening, crammed with some three hundred blue-blooded revellers, even the pilot was drunk, and a short way out, directly on the course to England, lay the shallow waters and swift currents of the Pointe de Barfleur, the rocky north-eastern extremity of Normandy's Cotentin Peninsula. Poorly guided, the ship struck the rocks, broke open its hull, and immediately heeled over and began to sink. Although the captain swiftly arranged for William the Atheling to transfer to the pilot boat, in their panic so many of the other nobility tried to follow that this in its turn sank under the weight. The only individual who lived to tell the tale was the poorest passenger on board, a butcher from Rouen.

The news of the disaster rocked the Norman court in much the same way that the loss of the *Titanic* would stun Edwardian England centuries later. There was scarcely an aristocratic family which did not have some young son or daughter on board, and Henry himself fainted when the news was eventually broken to him, by a child, as none of the adults dared. Not least of Henry's problems was that he had been left without a legitimate heir, and his wife had died two years before.

For us a particular interest of the tragedy lies in where off the Pointe de Barfleur the remains of the *White Ship* might lie. The sea-bed in this region is a veritable graveyard of many ships, some inevitably larger, more recent and more impressive than the vessel which carried William the Atheling, but none more historic. Expectations of finding the ship in any state of near-completeness are very remote, particularly in view of the turbulent and rocky nature of the waters around the Pointe de Barfleur. The same conditions add an extra hazard to the task of searching for the wreck. But given the status of the individuals who were on board, even if just a few of their personal belongings happened to find a haven in a soft patch of sea-bed these might offer a time-capsule glimpse of the Norman world of the twelfth century historically at least as rewarding, if not more so, than the Tudor world opened up by the *Mary Rose*.

The quest is one only for the most experienced and well-equipped, and most definitely not for the treasure-hunter. But it is to be hoped that someday it will be attempted.

SOURCES:

ORDERICUS VITALIS, In Duchesne, *Hist. Norm. Scriptt.*, pp. 868-9

CHAMBERS, James, *The Norman Kings*, London, Weidenfeld & Nicolson, 1981

THE SHIPS OF COLUMBUS

In any contest to decide the world's most historic ship, pride of place must surely go to the *Santa María*, the flagship of the diminutive trio of vessels with which Christopher Columbus made his historic discovery of the New World in 1492. The *Santa María* was neither a new nor a particularly impressive ship when Columbus gained command of her. A somewhat lumbering cargo-carrier of 100 tons (i.e., capable of holding 100 tons of wine), the name given to her by one of her previous masters was the *Marigalante*, or Naughty Mary, which Columbus promptly changed

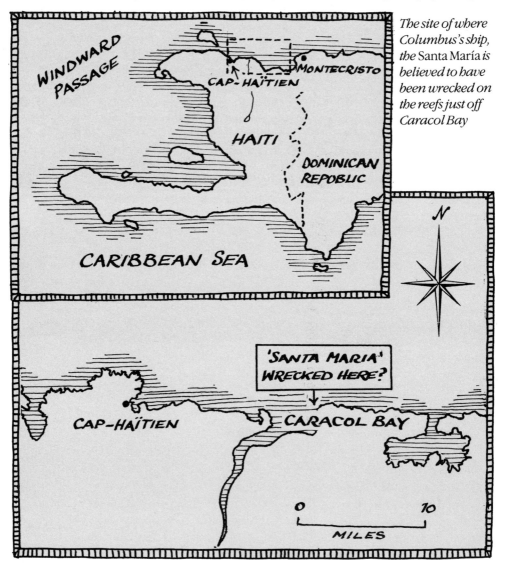

The site of where Columbus's ship, the Santa María *is believed to have been wrecked on the reefs just off Caracol Bay*

The historic moment of Columbus's first landfall in the Americas, from a sixteenth-century engraving

because of the seriousness of his mission. Although he did not change the name of his two other commands, these were similarly suspect, *La Pinta*, a 60-ton caravel, meaning 'The Painted One', or woman of easy virtue, and *La Niña*, of similar size, meaning 'The Girl'.

In modern terms all three vessels were no bigger, merely somewhat broader, than many of the larger yachts commonly found in harbours of the present-day. Yet, sailing literally into the unknown (more so than they knew), they managed the Atlantic crossing from the Canaries to the West Indies in just thirty-three days. Almost certainly their first landfall was the Bahamian island of San Salvador, where Columbus had his first historic meeting with natives from the New World. At Long Bay on this island archaeologists under the direction of Dr Charles Hoffman of Northern Arizona University have recently come across remains which would appear to be those of the original native village, complete with some of the cheap trinkets which Columbus brought as gifts.

After an encouraging reception – San Salvador's natives seem to have regarded Columbus and his men as literally from heaven – the three ships made their way onwards. First, they called in at Long Island in the Bahamas, then they went on to Cuba, where the *Pinta*'s captain decided to separate from the other two, then on to Hispaniola. For Columbus every new landfall brought fresh hopes that he had at last arrived at the goal he had set out for, the 'Cathay' of the Great Khan, which he had read about from Marco Polo.

Up to this point, with the exception of the defection of the *Pinta*, Columbus's expedition had proceeded almost flawlessly, particularly given the often treacherous nature of the waters into which it had sailed without the benefit of charts of any kind. The natives of Hispaniola proved as friendly as those they had met elsewhere, and on Christmas Eve 1492 after safely guiding *Santa María* and *Niña* past Hispaniola's towering Cap Haïtien, Columbus had every justification for relaxing overnight. The weather was fair and calm, *Niña* was leading the way, and on the flagship all Columbus's second-in-command Juan de la Cosa had to do was to follow. But Juan de la Cosa decided to hand over command to the ship's helmsman, who in turn handed over to one of the ship's boys. As Columbus subsequently recalled the incident:

> It pleased Our Lord that at midnight, while I lay in bed, with the ship in a dead calm and the sea as peaceful as the water in a cup, all went to sleep, leaving the tiller in charge of a boy. So it happened that the swells drove the ship very slowly onto one of those reefs, on which the waves broke with such a noise that they could be heard a long league away. Then the boy, feeling the rudder ground and hearing the noise, cried out; hearing him, I immediately arose, for I recognized before anyone else that we had run aground.

Although little time was lost in trying every nautical device to lever and float the *Santa María* free, it soon became apparent that she was stuck fast. Accordingly, it became Columbus's unhappy lot on Christmas Day to give the order for the vessel to be abandoned, and for all men and essential supplies to be transferred to the *Niña*, now the only ship left for the hazards of the return journey across the Atlantic.

But it was not possible for the two ships' companies to be carried in just the *Niña* for such a voyage, particularly since Columbus had already added to his charges by capturing some of the island's natives to show to his patrons King Ferdinand and Queen Isabella in Spain. So, the only available decision was for some forty of the crew to be left behind, equipped with food, weapons for protection and the necessary tools to transform salvaged timbers from the *Santa María* into a stockade village for themselves until an expedition could be mounted for their rescue. Given the pleasant West Indian climate and friendliness of the natives, Columbus found no shortage of volunteers for this venture. And as he reasoned to himself, perhaps the shipwreck had been deliberately intended by God to prompt him to found such a settlement as the first-ever European colony in this New World. Accordingly, with double appropriateness he called it La Na(ti)vidád, the Birthplace.

Just under two years later, this time with a complete flotilla of ships under his command, Columbus managed to find his way back to La Navidád, only to encounter evidence of a total disaster. From skeletons and from what the natives were able to tell him, he gradually learned how some of the men had set off into the interior in search of gold, only to meet up with a tribe of Indians with none of the friendliness of those on the coast. Not only had the gold-seekers been wiped out, their killers had then proceeded to La Navidád to overwhelm those who had stayed behind.

So what of the fate of the *Santa María*? La Navidád is known to have been east of Cap Haïtien, within the barrier reef of coral along that shore, not far from what is now called Caracol Bay, and therefore it must be presumed that if anything has remained of the world's most historic ship it is likely to be found somewhere there. But how completely was the ship dismantled to build the first colony? According to some, there is likely to be nothing left to discover. According to others, at least the shell of *Santa María* is likely to have survived. Currently, archaeologists from the University of Florida are actively trying to identify the site of La Navidád, and from this try to go on to pinpoint the remains of the *Santa María*, so only time can tell.

But, in any case, the *Santa María* was not the only ship that Columbus commanded and lost during his momentous, but increasingly disastrous, expeditions to the New World. In the course of his fourth and last voyage in 1502 the most serious hazard was shipworm which ultimately caused the loss of all four of the caravels with which Columbus had set out. The first two of these had to be stripped and scuttled in Panama, one of these the *Vizcaina*, being abandoned inside the harbour of Portobelo. The location of this was quite possibly identified in 1975 in the course of the British marine archaeologist Sydney Wignall's expedition to find Drake's coffin (see page 91), but it has yet to be excavated.

With all the crew members packed into his two remaining ships, *La Capitana* and *Santiago de Palos* Columbus tried to reach the Spanish base of Santo Domingo in what is today the Dominican Republic on Hispaniola. But off Cuba the ships were already literally sinking under their feet, and when they were beset by gales off the

Just outside Portobelo, Panama is the approximate site of where Columbus scuttled and abandoned the Vizcaina *during his expedition of 1502.*

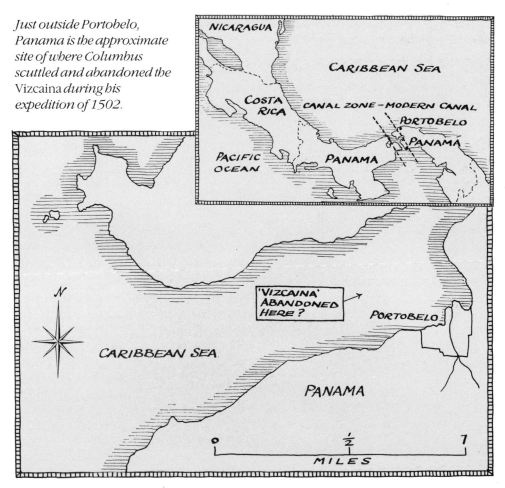

coast of Jamaica the situation became so desperate that on 29 June 1503 they had no option but to run aground about 'a crossbow shot from land' in St Ann's Bay, on Jamaica's northern coast. Only the ship's fore- and sterncastles remained above the water, and, unwilling to risk camping on the shore, yet reliant on food bartered with the natives, Columbus and the 116 members of his expedition were obliged to spend over a year in very uncomfortable circumstances.

Eventually, thanks to a heroic canoe voyage by one of the expedition's gentleman companions, Diego Méndez, rescue was arranged from Santo Domingo. But by this time Columbus had already suffered mutiny and was a sick and broken man. He would be dead within two years.

So given the fact that the spot where *La Capitana* and *Santiago de Palos* were beached is reasonably reliably known, is it possible still to trace these two wrecks? In 1940 a Harvard University expedition, led by the historian Samuel Eliot Morison failed to locate them, but in 1966 a second expedition led by the Florida marine archaeologist Robert F. Marx arrived in St Ann's Bay much better equipped. Using ten-foot metal probes to test for solid objects buried under the bay sediment, at a depth of eight feet they consistently hit a large solid object, which when a test hole

Robert Marx surfacing with timbers from one of the wrecks in St Ann's Bay, possibly from Columbus's ships, the Capitana *or the* Santiago de Palos

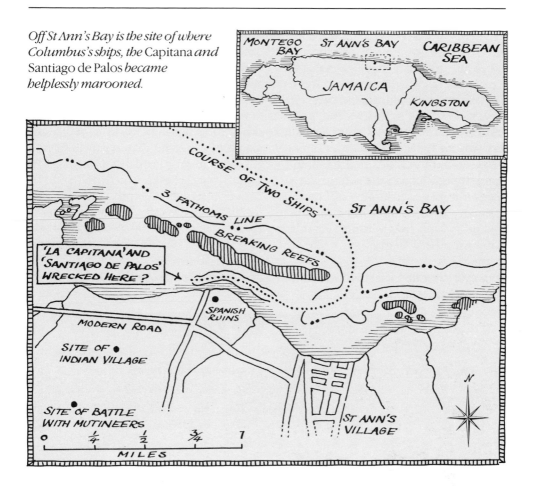

Off St Ann's Bay is the site of where Columbus's ships, the Capitana *and* Santiago de Palos *became helplessly marooned.*

was dug duly revealed a fragment of a ship's rib, and several pieces of obsidian, which Columbus's ships are specifically known to have been carrying among their various items of cargo.

Marx returned to the site two years later, this time accompanied by Dr Harold Edgerton of the Massachusetts Institute of Technology, famous for his invention of a special 'pinger' and 'boomer' form of sonar for mapping buried objects. Within an hour Edgerton's equipment located two sites in the bay, the first that had already been found by Marx, the second which was presumed to be the second of Columbus's beached caravels. The sonar profile of both features confirmed them to be shipwrecks, and in size and location they readily matched what would be expected of Columbus's *La Capitana* and *Santiago de Palos*. With the aid of a coring device supplied by Columbia University, specialists on Marx's team began extracting from the wrecks pieces of wood, glass and flint, iron nails and tacks, animal bones, ceramic sherds and beans, such finds strongly suggesting to them that these were from Columbus's ships and no other.

Problematically, investigations by Texas A & M University's Institute of Nautical Archaeology during the summers of 1982-6, using yet more sophisticated remote-sensing instruments, and further coring and test excavations, have revealed yet more historic wrecks in St Ann's Bay, confusing the issue of which might have been the ships belonging to Columbus. Furthermore, even if the Institute's specialists were able to satisfy themselves that they had located the correct ships, to extract *La Capitana* and *Santiago de Palos* from their muddy tomb would be a highly expensive undertaking. However, 1992 will be the 500th anniversary of Columbus's discovery of the Americas, and it would surely not be beyond the resources of a country as rich as the United States for such unique monuments of its past to be brought to light, perhaps by a dramatic raising in the same manner as England's *Mary Rose,* or perhaps by the building of a cofferdam, from which the water could be pumped out and the ships excavated as on dry land? Neither method would be easy. But if even just one of Columbus's ships could be brought to light in such a manner, it could provide a fascinating insight into the lives of those intrepid mariners who five hundred years ago sailed so optimistically westwards – and found the New World.

Dr Edgerton and Robert Marx examining part of the sub-bottom profiling sonar equipment

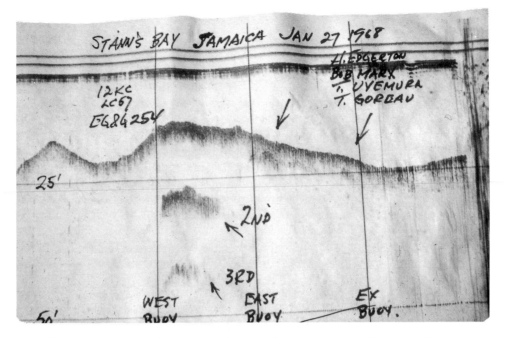

Dr Edgerton's sonar graph print-out, showing the sounding on which one of the Columbus ships may have been located. This is indicated by the smudge beyond the arrow labelled '2nd'.

SOURCES:

BRADFORD, Ernle, *Christopher Columbus*, London, Michael Joseph, 1973

MARX, Robert F., 'Shipwrecks in the wake of Columbus', article in MUCKELROY, Keith (Ed.), *Archaeology Under Water, An Atlas of the World's Submerged Sites*, New York & London, McGraw Hill, 1980

MORISON, Samuel Eliot, *Admiral of the Ocean Sea*, 2 vols., Oxford, Oxford University Press, 1940

SMITH, Roger C., and Donald H. Keith, 'Ships of Discovery', *Archaeology*, March/April 1986, pp. 30-35

WIGNALL, Sydney, *In Search of Spanish Treasure, A Diver's Story*, Newton Abbot, Devon, David & Charles, 1982, p. 218

SIR RICHARD GRENVILLE'S REVENGE

In the ranks of England's most historic fighting ships, a close second to the *Golden Hind* must be a ship also with associations with Sir Francis Drake, the 500-ton galleon *Revenge*, built in 1574. Measuring ninety-two feet in length and thirty-two in the beam, *Revenge* was by no means one of the largest of the English ships of her time, but she was certainly one of the nimblest and best armed. With a normal complement of 150 sailors, twenty-four gunners and seventy-six soldiers (the latter chiefly for boarding purposes), her gun decks bristled with twenty-two culverins and twelve light cannon. It was from *Revenge* that Sir Francis Drake captured the much larger Spanish galleon *Nuestra Señora de Rosario* during the repulse of the Spanish Armada in 1588, Drake's men taking over the Spanish ship while the Spanish commander Don Pedro de Valdez and his fellow-officers were brought as prisoners on board *Revenge*.

But the *Revenge*'s most dramatic, if fatal role was to come in 1591, after Drake had fallen from favour, when she was under the command of the fiery Sir Richard Grenville, cousin of Sir Walter Raleigh. Faced with their usual problem of how to safeguard the transport of yet another huge quantity of their annual haul of gold and silver from the New World, the Spanish had decided the year before to delay the

The most likely site for the historic wreck of the Revenge *is off the easternmost island of Terceira in the Azores.*

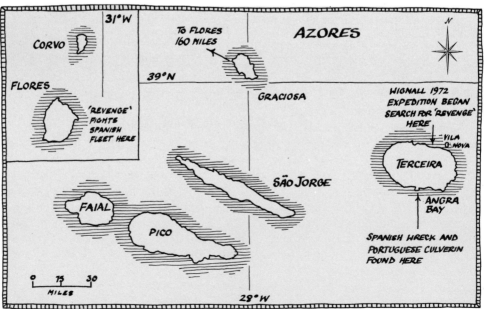

departure of their 1590 consignment in favour of a better protected double convoy organized for 1591. Having an efficient international intelligence service, the English not only learned of this but lost no time in putting together an interception fleet, with the somewhat effete Sir Thomas Howard as its admiral, and the far more able Grenville as his second-in-command. Knowing that en route to Spain the Spanish fleet would stop-over at the Azores in mid-Atlantic, seven English ships made their way to the westernmost Azores island of Flores, there to await first sight of a Spanish sail coming over the horizon.

The wait was unexpectedly long, giving rise to the first problem for the English, a serious outbreak of sickness, principally scurvy, brought on by the prolonged period at sea. Accordingly, many crew members were put ashore on Flores, to better recuperate there. But the second problem, unknown to the English was that the Spanish had in their turn learned of the English plan of interception, and had organized their own counter-interception mission, a formidable flotilla of fifty-three fighting galleons dispatched from Spain to the Azores under Captain General Don Alonzo de Bazan, there to catch the English as in a vice between the two fleets.

However, hardly had this flotilla left Spanish shores before it happened to be spotted by an English privateer commanded by George, third Earl of Cumberland, who, correctly anticipating the danger to his countrymen, had dispatched a fast pinnace, the *Moonshine*, to outrun Bazan and warn Howard and Grenville. *Moonshine* arrived at Flores just ahead of the Spanish, to find Howard so badly prepared that he could only order immediate evacuation, abandoning the sick still on shore. At least to Howard's credit he got all his ships away, and these being lighter and more manoeuvrable than their Spanish counterparts, they relatively easily managed to give the ambush the slip.

But Richard Grenville was not the sort of man to leave any of his crew to an uncertain fate at Spanish hands. With huge galleons bearing down on him he calmly loaded the last of the sick on board, and then, instead of hoisting full sail, proceeded at a deliberately restrained pace into the thick of the now inescapable oncomers.

The *Revenge* at that time had a complement of less than 300 seamen, and 39 guns. On the Spanish vessels were 7,000 Spaniards and Portuguese, armed with some 1,000 guns, one of the first into the attack being the 1,500-ton, 90-gun *San Felipe*, three times the size of the *Revenge*. Incredibly, *Revenge*'s first well-aimed broadside shot away the *San Felipe*'s rigging, crippling her so that she had to sheer away almost completely out of control.

Next into the confrontation was admiral Don Martin de Bertandona's *San Barnabe*, which grappled *Revenge*'s port side, while another attacked on the starboard, and yet another, that of Admiral Marcos de Aramburu, took on the *Revenge*'s bow. The *Revenge*'s starboard guns swiftly crippled the starboard attacker so that it slunk away to sink with almost all hands, while her two bow-chase guns toppled Aramburu's ship's rigging like a pack of cards, causing this too to drift helplessly away. As another galleon latched itself to the starboard, once again the English guns dealt her a lethal punishment, the vessel sinking almost immediately, although not without taking with her *Revenge*'s mainmast, which had at last succumbed to the Spanish pounding. In the midst of all this soldiers from the *San Barnabe* managed to fight their way onto *Revenge*'s deck, but were swept off this in a determined charge led by Grenville himself.

Now, however, the Spanish tried a new tactic. No less than two huge vessels fastened themselves to the *Revenge*'s starboard side, murderous exchanges of fire continuing into the night until, with the sheer weight of opposition and lack of ammunition the last few English guns began to fall silent.

By the break of a new day ninety English dead were laid out below *Revenge*'s decks, scarcely a man was not wounded, and the Spanish, genuinely impressed by such a display of heroism, were calling for an honourable surrender. But Grenville, mortally wounded, would have none of it, even giving orders for the *Revenge* to be blown up with the last remaining powder. In fact, these orders were counter-manded by some of his own surviving crew, and Grenville, taken on board the *San Barnabe*, breathed his last crushing between his teeth the very glass with which his captors tried to ply him with Spanish wine.

The gallant *Revenge* was now taken in tow, viewed with awe, along with the havoc she had wrought, by the plate fleet from the West Indies as this at last arrived. But this was not the end of Spanish misfortunes. As the combined fleets made their way to their agreed rendezvous point at the Azores island of Terceira, a fierce autumn storm blew up, sending more than twenty vessels to the bottom, including the *Revenge*, which struck rocks just off Terceira. She went down with all hands, many of these the Spanish and Portuguese crew who had taken her over. The solitary exception was an Englishman who managed to crawl ashore on Terceira to tell the story of her last moments. But he in his turn died shortly after.

So, it is somewhere off Terceira that the remains of the *Revenge* are likely to survive to this day, the difficulty, for those who want to find her, being exactly where she may have gone down. In 1972 the marine archaeologist Sydney Wignall, with the backing of Portuguese museum authorities, the Portuguese navy, and Britain's Council for Nautical Archaeology, mounted a well-equipped expedition to Ter-ceira, concentrating his attention to the Bay of Vila Nova, which has a vicious-looking reef on its outer limit. Some years earlier, at about this spot, according to what Wignall had learned from the museum authorities:

> . . . divers had carried out an illegal operation in locating two or more bronze guns on the reef, carrying them ashore at night, then smuggling them by boat to the mainland for sale to a private collector. The guns reputedly had a crest on the breech, and this crest was a flower. This I hypothesized could be the Tudor rose, which is always present on guns cast for Queen Elizabeth I.

Somewhat hampered by shoals of jellyfish, Wignall and his team systematically searched the reef area off Vila Nova Bay for several weeks during the early part of 1972, then proceeded to work their way around the island. In the Bay of Angra they found in shallow water an almost completely denuded ancient wreck with just a few cast iron guns remaining, which they identified as most likely a Spanish ship known to have sunk in 1608. At a separate site at a depth of seventy-five feet in the same bay they found another scattering of cast-iron cannon, again most likely Spanish, but with no clear traces of the ship from which these had come. As the team's permit was specific to the location, survey and excavation only of the *Revenge*, both finds were left to the Portuguese authorities, as was a magnificent fifteen-foot-long Portuguese bronze culverin dated 1545, found on the very last day.

During six months work the Wignall team explored about half of Terceira's coastal waters. But they failed in their attempt to locate *Revenge*, currently believed

ABOVE: The Revenge's *last battle, 31 August to 1 September 1591, from an engraving by A. Willmore, after a painting by D. W. Brierly. Under the command of the doughty Sir Richard Grenville (RIGHT) the* Revenge *took on single-handed virtually an entire armada of Spanish and Portuguese ships off the Azores in mid-Atlantic.*

Although Sydney Wignall's 1972 expedition unsuccessfully searched Terceira's waters for the Revenge, *they found instead this fifteen-foot Portuguese bronze cannon.*

by Wignall to lie in a particular complex of huge, jagged reefs. And so the discovery, if any such is to be made, still awaits a future expedition, which would need to apply for the same permits as those secured by Wignall. Since there was no time for anyone to strip the *Revenge* before she went down, she could be a most interesting wreck, preserving perhaps at least some of the traces of one of the most remarkable naval engagements in English history. And this, far more than any 'treasures' found on board, would be the value of any attempt to excavate her. Accordingly, the task is one to be attempted only by the most experienced professionals.

SOURCES:

BUSHNELL, G. H., *Sir Richard Grenville*, 1936

RALEIGH, W., *The Last Fight of the Revenge*

ROWSE, A. L., *Sir Richard Grenville of the Revenge, An Elizabethan Hero*, London, Cape, 1937

WIGNALL, Sydney, *Project Revenge*, private circulation, 1972

—, *In Search of Spanish Treasure, A Diver's Story*, Newton Abbot, Devon, David & Charles, 1982

SIR FRANCIS DRAKE'S GOLDEN HIND

If Columbus's *Santa María* has a just claim as perhaps the world's most historic ship, running a close second, at least in English eyes, must be Sir Francis Drake's *Golden Hind*, in which he made his round-the-world voyage in 1577.

Exactly who built the ship and when is unknown, but she was certainly not new when Drake took her over, at which time she was called the *Pelican*. Although no exact drawings or specifications have survived, her length is known to have been about a hundred feet and her displacement no more than 140 tons, small even by the standards of the time. But she was well armed, with seven guns either side, two on the poop and a number of smaller cannon. And she was sturdily built. According to a Portuguese pilot, Nuñō da Silva, who had some fifteen months' first-hand experience of life on board:

> Drake's ship is very stout and very strong, with double sheathing. . . . She is a French ship [i.e. built after the French fashion], well-fitted, with good masts, tackle and good sails, and is a good sailer, answering the helm well. She is neither new, nor is her bottom covered with lead. . . . She is staunch when sailing with the wind astern if it is not very strong, but in a sea which makes her labour she makes no little water.

This was the ship which on 15 November 1577 along with four other ships, the eighty-ton *Elizabeth*, the fifty-ton *Swan*, the thirty-ton *Marigold*, and the tiny pinnace *Christopher* left Plymouth under Drake's command for what was ostensibly a trip to Alexandria, but which according to Drake's secret instructions was to be a reconnoitre of the west coast of South America. After a brief return to Plymouth for repairs caused by storm damage, the fleet's first port of call was the Moroccan coast of Africa, where two Spanish caravels were captured, one of these being taken over in place of the pinnace *Christopher*, and given its name. The next stop-off was the Cape Verde islands, where a Portuguese cargo ship was taken over and re-named *Mary* after Drake's wife. It was in this episode that Drake acquired what were to be the very useful services of the pilot, Nuñō da Silva. Then, after of necessity revealing to the officers the expedition's true destination, it was on to South America, where land was sighted just north of the River Plate, after two months at sea.

As the fleet sailed southwards down the coast of Brazil keeping the ships together proved a difficulty. First the *Swan*, with the appropriate transfer of all crew and valuables, was abandoned in Seal Bay, Patagonia; then, in quick succession the *Christopher II* and the *Mary*. A further difficulty was disaffection among some of the gentlemen accompanying the voyage, one of these, Thomas Doughty, actively fomenting a mutiny against Drake's leadership. With an appropriateness not lost on his crews, Drake put into Port St Julian where Magellan fifty-eight years before had hanged mutineers against his leadership; they even managed to find the original gibbet. There, Drake formally tried and executed Doughty, pardoned others whom he knew to have been implicated, and in a test of his leadership stripped all officers of their rank, so that everyone on the voyage continued on an equal footing.

With minds suitably concentrated the expedition approached the Straits of Magellan, where in a brief further piece of showmanship Drake gave the *Pelican* its new name *Golden Hind* in honour of his patron, Sir Christopher Hatton, who had a golden hind as his coat of arms. The move was presumably to compensate for the fact that Drake had by now lost two vessels bearing Sir Christopher's Christian name. The fleet successfully emerged through the Strait and into the South Pacific, but there encountered such severe gales that they became separated, the *Marigold* disappearing without trace, and the *Elizabeth*, believing the *Golden Hind* also to be most likely lost, deciding to return for home back through the Magellan Straits.

But although the *Golden Hind* had been blown far to the south, she survived, in the process proving that there was open sea to the south of South America. With now simply a single ship under his command, and going where no English ship had gone before, Drake headed northwards up the coast of Chile, cheerfully raiding Spanish ports along the way. Off Peru he heard that there was a valuable cargo on its way to Panama, and catching up with the ship carrying this, the *Nuestra Señora de la Concepción* (better known by her nickname *Cacafuego*), he courteously transferred to the *Golden Hind*'s hold: 'fruits, conserves, sugars and a great quantity of jewels and precious stones, 13 chests of royals of plate, 80lb weight of gold [and] 26 tons of uncoined silver'.

Further prizes followed, including booty from a raid on the Guatemalan town of Guatulco, after which Drake headed northwards up the west coast of north America in the hope of finding a North-West passage back to England. Off Vancouver Island, however, having met increasingly colder conditions and no sign of a way eastward Drake wisely turned back south to the warmth of California, where the local Indians welcomed him as a god. At a spot which cannot be identified precisely, but which was most likely the present-day Drake's Bay just north of San Francisco Drake formally claimed California for the English crown, setting up a metal plaque (the disputed original is now in the University of California's Bancroft Library) which read:

> Be it known unto all men by these presents, June 17, 1579, by the Grace of God, in the name of Her Majesty Queen Elizabeth of England and Her successors for ever, I take possession of this Kingdom, whose King and people freely resign their right and title in the whole land unto Her Majesty's keeping, now named by me and to be known unto all men as Nova Albion.

Five weeks were spent refurbishing and re-victualling *Golden Hind*, after which Drake and his crew set sail eastwards across the Pacific. There were two months without sight of land, then followed various brushes with unfriendly islanders, before they eventually found themselves at Ternate in the Moluccas, or Spice Islands, where they were given a friendly welcome by the local Sultan. Further refurbishing was carried out on an uninhabited island, then it was on through the remaining Indonesian islands, where they hit their worst moment of danger, a submerged reef which held *Golden Hind* captive for twenty-four hours. Jettisoning of some of the cargo failed to shift her, but with a change of tide suddenly she floated free, and managed to reach Java, where there were friendly exchanges with the local Rajah.

Now there lay before *Golden Hind* the Indian Ocean, where again neither

A modern reconstruction of the Golden Hind *photographed at Tower Bridge, London in 1973. The remains of the original are thought to lie buried three miles downstream.*

Englishman nor English ship had ventured before. But by this stage the ship and its crew took what was to prove to be a two-month long haul almost in their stride, making a landfall near modern Durban in South Africa, then rounding the Cape of Good Hope on 15 June 1580 for the last leg of the journey, up the west coast of Africa. After a re-victualling stop just north of Sierra Leone, *Golden Hind* was off the

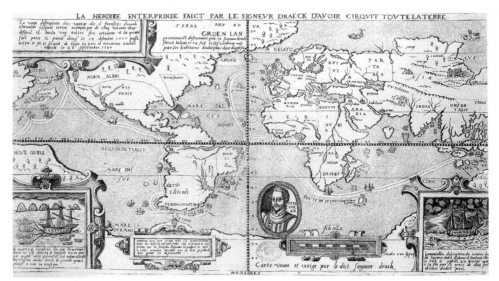

A map of Drake's circumnavigation of the world in the Golden Hind, *made by the Dutch engraver Nicola van Sype little more than three years after the* Golden Hind's *return*

Canaries on 22 August and on 26 September back home in Plymouth Sound. According to Drake's careful log-keeping the day should have been a Monday, but as he had failed to realize, he had lost a day in sailing round the world, and so it was a Sunday, and everyone was at church! The first-ever English circumnavigation of the world, dating from the second departure from Plymouth, had taken two years, nine months and thirteen days.

After such an unauspicious beginning – made worse by Plymouth being in the grip of a plague – Drake and his crew's welcome back home rapidly escalated to the rapturous, particularly when those who had sponsored his expedition became aware of the huge return on their investment which lay in the *Golden Hind*'s hold.

Each of Drake's backers made 4,700 times the amount of money they had originally put up to finance him, the Queen's share becoming the very foundation of subsequent British foreign investment. For Drake there was a knighthood, and for the *Golden Hind* also, a special honour. As reported to Philip II of Spain by his ambassador in London, Don Bernadino de Mendoza:

> She [Queen Elizabeth I] says she will knight him on the day she goes to see his ship, which she has ordered to be brought ashore and placed [at Deptford] as a curiosity.

So, in a final flourish, Drake and his crew sailed *Golden Hind* along the English Channel and up the Thames to Deptford, where on 4 April 1581 Drake duly received the accolade of knighthood. Queen Elizabeth was given a tour of inspection of the ship, after which in accordance with her instructions, a special dock was built nearby so that the *Golden Hind* could become a permanent tourist attraction, in the manner adopted more than two centuries later for Lord Nelson's flagship *Victory* at Portsmouth.

For some three generations *Golden Hind* remained on view at Deptford in the way Elizabeth I had decreed. In 1592 the Duke of Württemberg is recorded to have been shown over the ship, and in 1624 a special wharf was built nearby. But after 1662 the information becomes scanty, and it would appear that, in an age less conscious of conservation than our own, souvenir hunters simply chipped away at too many of the timbers, so that the *Golden Hind*, stoutly built though she was, became reduced to a shadow of her former glory. According to some accounts, she was reduced still further by a fire which gutted her to the waterline, as a result of which interest in and awareness of her whereabouts faded even more.

Then in November 1912 some construction workers working on an extension to Woolwich power station, just down-river from the former royal dockyard, came across the remains of an old timber warship which at first was identified as from the eighteenth century, and of very little interest. Accordingly, during 1913, which proved to be a very hot summer, the timbers were simply prised out of the mud (which had preserved them very well), and left lying in the sun, whereupon they soon began to disintegrate. Only when it was virtually too late did anyone realize that the ship was some centuries older than had previously been thought, and could conceivably be the *Golden Hind*. Typical were these reminiscences of a correspondent to *The Times*, a Mr Bertram Carter, on 3 August 1963:

> I was taken to see her by Mr Castle of the famous ship breakers firm, and I took some photographs with my box quarter-plate camera which unhappily were destroyed in the last war. Her ribs were of English oak, 16 inches by 16 inches, grown to shape and set 16 inches apart. Her outer and inner plankings were 6 inch and 4 inch respectively giving an all over thickness to the hull of

The last resting-place of the Golden Hind*? Her timbers are most likely to be found amid the remains of Deptford's seventeenth-century naval dockyard, yet to be excavated.*

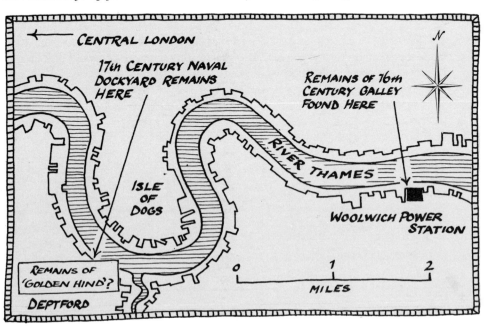

26 inches. . . . The keelsons were shaped out of single pieces of oak 16 inches thick, 8 foot long and 6 foot wide, the ribs being secured between them. Her mainmast was formed of an octagonal centre core 12 inches across with eight radiating sections and bound with iron hoops. Some stone, presumably shot, was found of different sizes. Her foremast and bow still lie under the power house unless it has been rebuilt.

But although Carter and others were convinced that the remains were those of the *Golden Hind*, in fact this is most unlikely, for two reasons. First, the historical sources are explicit that the *Golden Hind*'s last resting-place was Deptford, not Woolwich, even though these locations are relatively close to each other. Second, at least the dimensions of the Woolwich ship were noted in 1913, and it is quite apparent that it was significantly larger than the 100-foot length and 18-foot beam known of the *Golden Hind*. Probably the Woolwich ship was the *Great Galley*, a 120-oar, Venetian-style vessel which appears in the naval service records between 1515 and 1562, and which in its own right should have been accorded far more historical interest than it received.

As a result this renews the mystery of the *Golden Hind*'s whereabouts – or almost. For in October 1977, intrigued to determine the fate of one of the most historic vessels of all time, the archaeologist Peter Marsden of the Museum of London conducted a trial excavation at a site close to the Pepys Library at Deptford. He has yet to publish a report of his excavation, but has at least disclosed the following in a letter to the author:

> . . . I did excavate very close to the *Golden Hind* site in Deptford, but was restricted by the openings in the riverside paved area at Deptford Strand. There was no ship in the area of our trench, but we did encounter large quantities of tar and wood shavings dating from the early 17th century. This links up with what we know – that the ship was under the control of the naval dockyard at that time. The historical evidence links the site to a small area, and because the ground is somewhat waterlogged there is reason to believe that the lower part of the ship will have survived. It will be only on a future excavation, when the area for excavation is not restricted by blocks of flats and large paved areas, that there will be a chance of finding the hull.

So the encouraging news, particularly given the short life of many modern London blocks of flats, is that one day at least some substantial part of one of the most historic ships of all time could be retrieved for posterity. Although no doubt there will be technical difficulties, it seems an opportunity not to be missed, and a rather more worthy memorial than what has remained of *Golden Hind* so far, a table in London's Inner Temple and a chair in Oxford's Bodleian Library, both reputed to have been made from her scrap timbers.

SOURCES:

WILLIAMS, Neville, *Francis Drake*, London, Weidenfeld & Nicolson, 1974

Letter from Mr Bertram Carter, *The Times*, 3 August 1963

Correspondence with Mr Peter Marsden of the Museum of London

JOHN PAUL JONES'S
BONHOMME RICHARD

A story rarely taught in English history, but well known to almost every American schoolchild, is that of the naval commander John Paul Jones and his ship the *Bonhomme Richard*, who together took part in one of the most colourful episodes in the American War of Independence.

Born in Scotland in 1747, Jones was originally known simply as John Paul, and only adopted his subsequent surname on settling in Virginia after an early career as

John Paul Jones, the American War of Independence hero, was commander of the United States' first flagship, the Bonhomme Richard.

The height of the engagement between the Bonhomme Richard *and the British frigate* Serapis

a sailor. Once a colonist Jones quickly grew to resent the injustices of the prevailing British rule, and when in 1775 the rebel Congress resolved to equip a navy, he offered his maritime experience to the new cause.

Given command of a brig of eighteen guns, Jones early on established his bravery in exploits around the British coast, and in 1779 was appointed commander of a squadron of five vessels, two French and three American, to carry on similar harassing of shipping around British waters. On 23 September in his veteran flagship the former French merchantman *Bonhomme Richard*, Jones and his companions sighted and began to intercept a forty-one strong convoy of British merchant vessels plying the Baltic trade route just off Flamborough Head on the Yorkshire coast. Protecting the convoy were two large and well-armed British frigates, the forty-gun *Serapis*, commanded by Captain Richard Pearson, and the twenty-gun *Countess of Scarborough*. There followed a fierce naval engagement during which Jones's *Bonhomme Richard* began to lose the day, riddled with holes below the waterline, with four feet of water in the hold, and all but three of her guns silenced. The *Serapis* pulled alongside the *Bonhomme Richard*, and amid the smoke and confusion Captain Pearson could be heard calling for Jones's surrender: 'Have you struck?'

But surrender was the last thing Jones had in mind. 'I have not yet begun to fight', he yelled in reply. Lashing his ship to the *Serapis*, he and his men leapt on board, and in the course of fierce hand-to-hand fighting, completely overpowered the British crew. The *Bonhomme Richard* eventually sank after some thirty hours of drifting up and down with the tide, but Jones now had the *Serapis* at his disposal, and with the Union Jack struck from her mainmast, he and his crew successfully escaped with her to the Dutch island of Texel.

Jones subsequently went to Paris, where he died in 1792 in the midst of the events of the French Revolution, and for many years there was mystery concerning the wherabouts of his grave. After a search instituted by the American ambassador General Horace Porter in 1905 it was traced to the old St Louis cemetery in Paris. From there Jones's remains were exhumed and conveyed by the American navy to Annapolis, Maryland where they were reburied with full military honours in the Naval College's church crypt.

But of the remains of the *Bonhomme Richard*, historic as America's first flagship, so far there has been found no trace, or at least, almost no trace. Mindful of the vessel's significance for American citizens, in 1975 the British marine archaeologist Sydney Wignall instigated the first serious attempt to try to relocate the vessel. After considerable difficulties, in 1976 he managed to obtain a funding of $10,000, and the loan of a 200-ton hydrographic research vessel, the sonar-equipped *Decca Recorder*, as the only 'non-American' venture sponsored by the American government to mark the Bicentennial of American Independence.

From historical sources, and prevailing knowledge of marine conditions a computer study indicated the likeliest area for the wreck's location as a four-mile wide by six-mile long area of sea-bed just to the north-east of Flamborough Head. A

North-east of Flamborough Head, off the north Yorkshire coast of England, lies the area in which the Bonhomme Richard *could one day be found.*

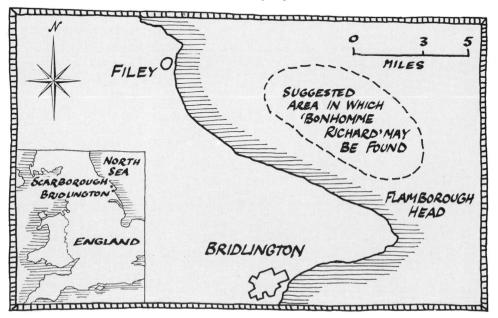

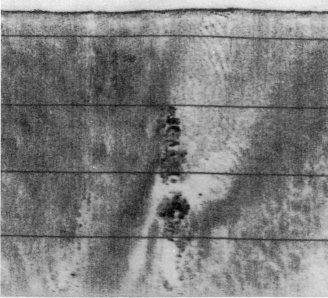

ABOVE: this French musket fished from the sea five miles off Flamborough Head could possibly have come from the Bonhomme Richard.

LEFT: This nearby sonar trace may represent a much-broken up Bonhomme Richard but the Wignall expedition of 1976 was not equipped for direct diving to check this out.

further chance pinpointing seemed to be provided by the fisherman John Pockley's unexpected 'catch', while long-line fishing five miles off Flamborough Head, of a muzzle-loading flintlock musket with a brass breech-plate bearing the date 1774. Since such a musket was quite uncharacteristic of the English Royal Navy's weaponry of the period, Wignall surmised that the musket was most likely French, and probably belonged to one of the French marines who formed part of the *Bonhomme Richard*'s crew.

Wignall therefore concentrated the *Decca Recorder*'s survey on the area of sea-bed indicated by the musket discovery. Here the side-scan sonar signalled several wrecks – the Royal Navy's Hydrographic Office in Bath has a list of some two hundred known off the coast between Bridlington and Scarborough – including, almost at the very spot of the musket discovery, the substantial iron hulk of the SS *Commonwealth*, a First World War freighter sunk by a German U-boat in 1918. None of the wrecks located were even remotely identifiable as the *Bonhomme Richard*, and Wignall was sadly obliged to call off his search after five and a half working days because this was all the time his free loan arrangement allowed. As he has since surmised, if the wreck of the wooden *Bonhomme Richard* lies where he believes it to be, 175 feet down and in close proximity to that of the *Commonwealth*, any signals from the former would almost inevitably be completely overshadowed by those of the latter. If he is right any eventual location of John Paul Jones's ship will need more sophisticated detection apparatus and a longer survey time.

Since Wignall's attempt there has been another unsuccessful venture, an all-American one of two weeks' duration, financed and led by Clive Cussler, author of *Raise the Titanic*, in 1979. And in 1986 Commander Derek Haggerston, head of Scarborough Sea Cadet Corps, planned to lead a team of some twenty cadets and deep-sea divers in a search concentrated on a spot twenty miles out to sea, between Flamborough Head and Filey Brig. He has selected this location from information he has found in possibly crucial vintage naval charts pinpointing shipwreck locations, one of these dating back to the year 1800. If the Scarborough Sea Cadet venture is successful they stand to receive a reward of £20,000 which Clive Cussler has promised to anyone who ultimately finds the *Bonhomme Richard*.

But simply finding the wreck will clearly not be enough. Could it be sufficiently well preserved for it to be methodically excavated and raised like the *Mary Rose*? Might sufficient American patriotic fervour be aroused for it to be transported – with appropriate British permission – back to the United States, perhaps to join the body of John Paul Jones in Annapolis, Maryland?

SOURCES:

MORISON, S. E., *John Paul Jones: A sailor's biography*, London, Faber, 1960

WIGNALL, Sydney, 'Project *Bonhomme Richard*', *Proceedings of the Atlantic Charter Maritime Archaeological Foundation*, 1976

—, *In Search of Spanish Treasure, A Diver's Story*, Newton Abbot, Devon, David & Charles, 1982, pp. 221-226

'Sea cadets hope to raise 1779 warship', *The Times*, 30 December 1985

Part IV

Undiscovered
Treasure

For centuries men have been spurred on by dreams of finding buried or sunken treasure. Once it was the already rich who went off on such quests, as in the case of Heinrich Schliemann, who in the course of destructive, poorly documented excavations found gold on the site of Troy. Today the man-in-the-street armed with a cheap metal-detector can follow in Schliemann's clumsy footsteps, much to the chagrin of the professional archaeologist.

But historic items of gold or silver can be worth far more for their interest value and aesthetic beauty than merely their weight as shiny metal. The quest for these can be an honourable one, and help solve ancient, and even sometimes modern mysteries. These are just some that might appeal to the more responsible treasure hunter . . .

TREASURES OF HOMER'S TROY?

 Much as we think we live in enlightened times, in fact the twentieth century has been little less hazardous than earlier ages for priceless antiquities disappearing in times of war. In 1945, during the closing moments of the Second World War, there vanished one of the most highly publicized archaeological finds of the nineteenth century, the so-called 'Treasure of Priam', found by the self-made millionaire Heinrich Schliemann in the course of his excavations of the Turkish mound he thought to be ancient Troy.

The story of Schliemann's search for Troy is an epic which has been told many times, not always too accurately. In the middle of the nineteenth century many scholars were of the opinion that Homer's story of the Trojan War was a wild legend, without any serious historical foundation. Among those who believed there might have been a place called Troy, the favoured site was one near a tiny Turkish village called Bunarbashi. In Germany Schliemann, fascinated since boyhood by the Homer story, would seem to have followed along with the general view.

In 1868, however, Schliemann happened to meet the English-born American vice-consul Frank Calvert, who owned part of a pottery-strewn Turkish mound called Hisarlik, overlooking the Dardanelles Strait. Calvert, who had already tried to persuade the British Museum to fund a 'dig' at the site, told Schliemann that he had found in trial probings at Hisarlik 'the ruins and debris of temples and palaces which succeeded each other over long centuries'. Soon Calvert had so convinced Schliemann that Hisarlik was the site of Troy that the entrepreneurial German began unashamedly claiming the identification as his own.

By April 1870 Schliemann had obtained from the Turkish government permission to dig the part of the mound not owned by Calvert. In the course of the next three years he proceeded to excavate here in such a destructive manner – with a disregard for all levels he thought not to be Homeric – that Calvert was soon to regret ever having let the German into his confidence. Identifying (wrongly) among the archaeological strata Hisarlik's second level of occupation as that of Homeric Troy, Schliemann put forward as the proof of his claims the discovery of a remarkable hoard of gold ornaments, the 'Treasure of Priam'. According to his own account of how he found this hoard:

> I came upon a large copper article of the most remarkable form, which attracted my attention all the more and I thought I saw gold behind it. . . . I cut out the treasure with a large knife, which it was impossible to do without the very greatest exertion and the most fearful risk of my life, for the great fortification-wall, beneath which I had to dig, threatened every moment to fall down on me. But the sight of so many objects, every one of which is of inestimable value to archaeology, made me foolhardy, and I never thought of any danger. It would, however, have been impossible for me to have removed the treasure without the help of my dear wife [Greek-born Sophie Schliemann], who stood by me ready to pack the things which I cut out in her shawl and to carry them away.

Schliemann's 'Treasure of Priam' – smuggled from Turkey in the mistaken belief that it belonged to the period of Homer's Troy. One of the most famous of archaeological finds, it disappeared from Berlin at the end of the Second World War.

Although endlessly vaunted since as one of the 'great' moments in world archaeology, in fact, as Schliemann subsequently admitted to an English visitor, Thomas Borlase, Sophie Schliemann was not only not present at the time of the discovery, she was not even in the same country. The treasure was real enough, comprising gold, silver, electrum and bronze drinking cups, vases, a gold 'sauce-boat', gold bracelets, a gold headband, four beautiful earrings, two magnificent gold diadems, and several thousand gold rings and similar ornaments. But in view of Schliemann's outright lie over his wife's presence, there has to be some doubt

FACING PAGE: the German-born Heinrich Schliemann, a successful self-made millionaire and disastrous archaeologist.

RIGHT: The Greek-born Sophie Schliemann, provocatively wearing the so-called 'Jewels of Helen' which her husband smuggled from Turkey. For the unscholarly, this photograph was regarded as proof that Schliemann had found Homer's Troy.

BELOW: Part of the mound Hisarlik, probably correctly identified by Schliemann as Troy, but so inexpertly excavated by him that he all but destroyed the remains of the true Homeric period.

whether he genuinely found the items as a single hoard, or whether they were amassed over several weeks from various locations on the site.

For this was not the only respect in which Schliemann behaved less than honestly and honourably over the find. Instead of declaring it while he was in Turkey, which under the terms of his permit would have necessitated him handing over half to the Turkish government, he smuggled it out of the country via the American consul's diplomatic bag, and only announced it once it was (relatively) safe in Athens. To add to Turkish anger at his perfidy, he had his wife photographed wearing some of the jewellery. Labelled as 'the Jewels of Helen', it was possibly this photograph which more than any other convinced popular opinion that Homer's Troy had indeed been found, and that Schliemann was its discoverer.

For some time Schliemann was under considerable pressure to return the hoard to the Turks. In order to foil Turkish agents from retrieving it by force he had to disperse the various items among his wife's relatives. And he lost a legal action which the Turkish government brought against him in Athens, resulting in him being fined 50,000 francs which he paid five times over in the hope that his excavation permit (inevitably withdrawn) might eventually be renewed.

Eventually all the fuss died down, and after an appropriate space of years Schliemann donated the 'Treasure of Priam' to the Berlin Ethnological Museum. There it remained until the Second World War. But in the closing stages of the war, as Nazi fortunes began to wane, there were fears for its safety. First, it was moved to the Prussian State Bank. The next move was to the air-raid shelter at Berlin Zoo. Then, as the Allies closed in on Berlin the decision was taken to disperse it, along with a variety of other treasures, to various points of supposed safety: the Lebus Palace on the Polish border, Schönebeck on the Elbe in present-day East Germany, and the Petrusche Palace near Wroclaw in present-day Poland. There is no known record of which one of these it went to, but wherever, it disappeared amid the confusion of the final moments of the war – and has never been heard of again.

According to some rumours, it lies in a sealed vault in Leningrad. According to

The hunt for the 'Treasure of Priam'. This map shows where the Nazis hid some treasures in the closing days of the Second World War but where the 'Treasure of Priam' is now demands some exceptional sleuthing.

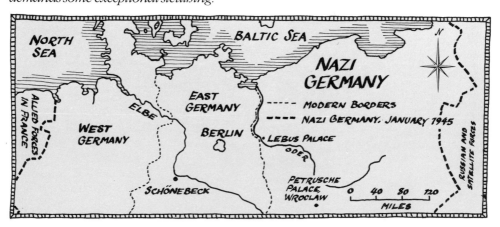

others it is in the secret collection of a Texas oil millionaire. There appears little of substance in either of these, and given the desperate state of many individuals at the end of the war, there has to be a strong likelihood that it ended up melted down for some refugee Nazi's pension fund.

So, short of some unexpected re-discovery, the antiquities that Schliemann contrived so hard to secure for western 'safe-keeping' remain lost without trace. Unfortunately for Schliemann's so-confident claims for them, their original owners never were any of the participants in Homer's Trojan War. In his over-eagerness, Schliemann had dug through the genuine Homeric level, destroying most of what he came across, the jewels being from a period of almost a thousand years before. Nonetheless, if they could be found they would still be of very considerable historical interest.

The irony of the story is that if only the British Museum had listened to Frank Calvert when he first approached them to fund an excavation at Hisarlik (which was in 1863, five years before Schliemann came on the scene), not only might the site of Troy have been better excavated (for scholars still argue about Schliemann's findings), the 'Treasure of Priam' might well have ended up in London, and be on view to this day.

SOURCES:

WOOD, Michael, *In Search of the Trojan War*, London, BBC Publications, 1985, pp. 47-61

HALL, A. R., 'The Recovery of Cultural Objects Dispersed During World War II', *Dept. of State Bulletin*, 27 August 1951

DUEL, Leo, *Memoirs of Heinrich Schliemann: a documentary portrait drawn from his autobiographical writings, letters and excavation reports*, London, Hutchinson, 1978

EASTON, Donald F., & David A. Traill, 'Schliemann's discovery of "Priam's treasure", two enigmas', *Antiquity*, vol. 55, 215, Nov. 1981, pp. 179-183, and vol. 57, 221, Nov. 1983, pp. 181-6

THE TREASURE OF THE
DEAD SEA SCROLLS

The story of how in 1947 a Bedouin boy called Moham-
med chanced upon a hoard of the famous 'Dead Sea
Scrolls' while searching for a lost goat is now one of
archaeology's legends. As soon as the Bedouin around
the Dead Sea realized that there was money to be made
from odd bits of old writing occasionally to be found in
their local caves, there was an inevitable scramble to find more, bringing to light a
whole gamut of scrolls that are still being studied by scriptural scholars.

Five years passed before in 1952 an official French and American expedition

*The terrain of the Dead Sea Scrolls, with some of the sites that may be mentioned in the
enigmatic Copper Scroll*

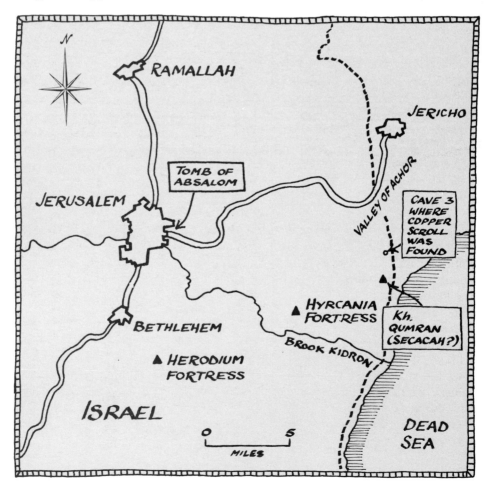

A mere notch in the barren hillside, one of the caves in which some of the so-called Dead Sea Scrolls were found

arrived to make an exhaustive survey of the caves, hoping to find at least something that the Bedouin might have overlooked. The work was unpleasant, involving scrabbling amid cooking dust in cramped caves in temperatures around 100 degrees Fahrenheit, and the expedition met with scant success apart from in what is now known as cave No. 3. Situated not far from the remains of the Qumran monastery whose community had owned the scrolls, this cave was one that had suffered a roof collapse in antiquity. Its floor was found to be littered with the now-characteristic fragments of scroll and broken pieces of the jars in which these had been stored originally.

But the real discovery was that of two rolled-up copper strips lying close up against an inner wall. These obviously contained writing, because indentations from Aramaic or Hebrew lettering on the underside could be clearly seen on the outermost portions of the rolls. But because of the effects of time the metal was severely oxidized so that any attempt to unroll the strips to read what was on them caused the handled portions simply to crumble to dust.

For four years there was much scientific head-scratching on the best method to

The two heavily oxidized rolls that comprised the Copper Scroll, seen as they were found in Cave No. 3

retrieve the all-important writing on the rolls. Although at Johns Hopkins University in Baltimore, American advances had been made in reconstituting corroded metals, the Dead Sea copper seemed too far gone for this. Accordingly a reluctant decision was made to cut the metal into strips using a cutting machine devised by Professor H. Wright Baker of the Engineering department of the Manchester College of Technology in Britain. With the help of an Araldite plastic coating to keep any fragmenting material in place, the operation was eventually successfully accomplished, revealing strip by strip the full hidden text for the first time since the original single document, which we may now call the Copper Scroll, had been rolled up nearly two thousand years ago.

The first surprise was that the document turned out to be the only non-religious document recovered from the writings of the Qumran community. The second surprise was that it seemed to be what every fortune-hunter has ever dreamed of, a guide to more than sixty hiding-places of buried treasure, apparently to be found in or near various tombs, cisterns, canals and underground passages scattered throughout the Judaean countryside.

Moreover, the volume of the buried treasure seemed to be vast, according to one decipherment, over 3,000 talents of silver, nearly 1,300 talents of gold, 65 bars of gold, 608 pitchers containing silver, and 619 silver and gold vessels, or in modern terms 65 tons of silver and 26 tons of gold. But as is the case with so many would-be treasure hunts, the Copper Scroll was not any immediate *open sesame* to undreamed-of riches.

Not least of the difficulties is the fact that the translation of such an ancient document is subject to differing interpretations. While everyone is agreed that the document is a list of at least some amount of buried treasure, according to one scholar, J. T. Milik, the list is a fictitious one, merely a compilation of legends of hidden gold and silver. For others, however, the treasure is considered to have been, and perhaps still is, very real. The sect responsible for the Dead Sea scrolls is thought to have been the Essenes mentioned by the first century AD Jewish historian Josephus, and since they were obliged to hand over their individual wealth to the community, the French scholar A. Dupont-Sommer has suggested that the treasure was or is their collective fortune, which they were obliged to hide during the savage Roman suppression of the first Jewish revolt around AD 68. According to another school of thought, that of K. G. Kuhn and Chaim Rabin, the treasure was or is what the Jews managed to rescue of the fortune of the Temple of Jerusalem, looted and razed to the ground by the Romans in AD70. Adding credence to the idea that a real treasure was involved is the fact that the document was created on an unusual and expensive material, copper, with the apparent clear intention that it should last. Indeed, it seems to have been rather rapidly transcribed from an earlier leather or papyrus scroll, as if at some time of crisis, with this very thought in mind.

But even if the fortune was or is a real one, a further difficulty lies in the fact that the apparent clues relate to locations which might have been relatively obvious back in the first century AD, but which in most cases seem to have long since vanished. And just how difficult it is to determine what the document is saying is quite apparent from the major discrepancies between the two main scholarly translations, those by J. T. Milik and those by his rival, Manchester University's controversial Oriental studies specialist, J. M. Allegro. The extent of the problem is quite apparent from the following extracts:

J. T. MILIK

(1) At Horebbeh which is in the valley of Achor, under the steps which go eastward, (dig) forty cubits; a chest (full) of silver weighing altogether seventy talents.

(2) In the sepulchral monument of Ben Rabbah the Shalishian: 100 bars of gold.

(3) In the great cistern which is in the Court of the little Peristyle which is closed with a pierced stone, in a recess of its base facing the upper opening: nine hundred talents.

J. M. ALLEGRO

(1) In the fortress which is in the Vale of Achor, forty cubits under the steps entering to the east; a money chest and its contents, of a weight of seventy talents.

(2) In the sepulchral monument in the third course of stones: light bars of gold.

(3) In the Great Cistern which is in the Court of the Peristyle, in the plaster of its floor, concealed in a hole in front of the upper opening: nine hundred talents.

(4) On the hill of Kohlit, jar(s) of aromatics, sandalwood, and sacred garments; all the aromatics and treasure; seven and one tenth (talents). Locate from the entrance of its revolving door the north of the exit of the canal (and count) six cubits towards the immersion pool.

(4) In the trough (?) of the Place of the Basin (?); tithe vessels, consisting of *log* vessels and amphorae, all of tithe and stored Seventh-Year produce and Second Tithe, from (the) mouths to the opening, and in the bottom of the water conduit, six cubits from the north towards the hewn immersion pool.

(64) In the gallery of the Smooth Rock north of Kohlit, opening to the north with tombs at its entrance: a copy of this document with the explanations and measurements and a detailed description.

(61) In the Pit adjoining on the north, in a hole opening northwards, and buried at its mouth: a copy of this document, with an explanation and their measurements, and an inventory of each thing, and oth[er things].

Some features in the Copper Scroll, common to both the Milik and Allegro versions, are recognizable. For instance, the 'vale of Achor' is referred to in association with the Dead Sea in Joshua 15:7, and is identified in biblical atlases as a valley among the hills just to the west of Qumran. Furthermore, this region does happen to have featured one of the major fortresses of the period first century BC to first century AD, Herod the Great's Hyrcania, which can be located on the hill now known as Khirbet Mird. But the Hyrcania's building blocks were re-used for a monastery, so not only has its exact plan been obscured, the Copper Scroll's 'chest (full) of silver weighing altogether seventy talents' might well have been found during the course of that rebuilding work.

However, such thoughts are not for the faint-hearted. The ruins are covered with huge amounts of sand, and since there has been no proper modern excavation of the site, it is just possible that this part of the Copper Scroll's treasure is traceable and does still exist.

Another name that is referred to in connection with no less than six of the Copper Scroll locations is Secacah, also mentioned in Joshua 15:61, where it is described as 'in the wilderness'. Here, Allegro has done some careful detective work comparing biblical place-names with some of those traditional to sites around the Dead Sea, and has concluded: 'the only real possibility of our Secacah is Khirbet Qumran itself, the site of the Essene monastery. Not only do the details of the scroll's description coincide remarkably well with what we find in the excavated settlement; but it has recently been shown that the Essenes built their desert home on much earlier remains, dating from Old Testament times.'

If this identification is correct – and it is one tentatively being made in modern biblical atlases – of particular potential is the reference to the tomb containing thirty-two talents of silver in the Wadi Kippa, along 'the eastern road to Secacah', as described in paragraph 25. According to Allegro, 'The eastern road to Secacah must be the track leading to the monastery plateau from the coast, parallel with the last furlongs of the Wadi Qumran'. If Allegro's deduction is correct, the tomb containing the silver might not be altogether beyond re-location.

Finally, another highly tantalizing passage is paragraph 49 with its mention of eighty talents buried at twelve cubits depth on the western side of the 'Monument of Absalom'. To this day the visitor to Jerusalem is able to see on the left-hand side of the road to Jericho a tomb called 'Absalom's Tomb', which seems to be carved out of

The 'Tomb of Absalom' in Jerusalem on the road to Jericho. Could this be the same as the 'Monument of Absalom' referred to in the Copper Scroll?

the mountainside. The structure certainly does not date from the time of Absalom, son of the biblical king David, being most likely of the much later first century BC/AD period. But it may well stand on the site of a much earlier, perhaps authentic tomb of the same individual, the name thus perpetuating a genuine ancient memory. As noted by the American popular writer Rene Noorbergen:

> The rocks immediately surrounding the tomb do not show any evidence of a shaft or a tunnel in which eighty talents of silver could have been hidden, but at a distance of sixteen yards from the tomb on the western side is an opening to a cistern which is said to be more than ten cubits deep and is said to run in the direction of the tomb. The shaft itself is empty, but is it possible that the treasure is hidden somewhere at the end of the shaft?

As is evident from the final paragraph, No. 64 in Milik's version and 61 in Allegro's, an apparently vital extra ingredient in any hunt for the treasure of the Copper Scroll is the 'copy of this document with the explanations and measurements and a detailed description' which is supposed to be found in the 'Gallery of the Smooth Rock north of Kohlit' according to Milik, or in the 'Pit adjoining on the north, in a hole opening northwards', according to Allegro. If there really is any of the Copper Scroll's lost treasure still waiting to be discovered, not least of any searcher's requirements will be the need for an appropriate permit from the antiquity-sensitive Israeli authorities, and, equally vital, choice of the correct translation!

SOURCES:

ALLEGRO, John Marco, *The Treasure of the Copper Scroll*, London, Routledge and New York, Doubleday, 1960

—, *The Dead Sea Scrolls*, London, Penguin, 1956

DUPONT-SOMMER, A., *The Essene Writings from Qumran*, Oxford, 1961

MILIK, J. T., 'Le Rouleau de Cuivre de Qumran', *Revue Biblique*, 1959, pp. 321-57

NOORBERGEN, Rene, *Treasures of the Lost Races*, New York, Bobbs-Merrill Co. Inc., 1982

VERMES, Geza, *The Dead Sea Scrolls in English*, London, Penguin, 1970 and Philadelphia, Fortress Press, 1981

KING JOHN'S 'JEWELS'

One of the best-known stories in English history is that of King John, Richard the Lionheart's wicked brother, supposedly losing his jewels in the Wash, the squarish inlet of sea between the counties of Norfolk and Lincolnshire.

The incident is dated to the year 1216, the last of King John's reign, and is described in the work of several early chroniclers. An account is found in Roger of Wendover's *Flores Historiarum*, written within a few years of the latter's death in 1235:

> Then, heading for the north, he [John] lost, by an unexpected accident, all the wagons, carts and packhorses, with the treasures, precious vessels, and all the other things which he cherished with special care; for the ground was opened in the midst of the waves, and bottomless whirlpools engulfed everything, together with men and horses, so that not a single foot-soldier got away to bear tidings of the disaster to the king. The king, however, barely escaping with his army, spent the following night at the abbey called Swineshead.

The Wash on the east coast of England, with the three likeliest sites for the loss of King John's baggage train. Since the area is now dry land might the valuables be relocated?

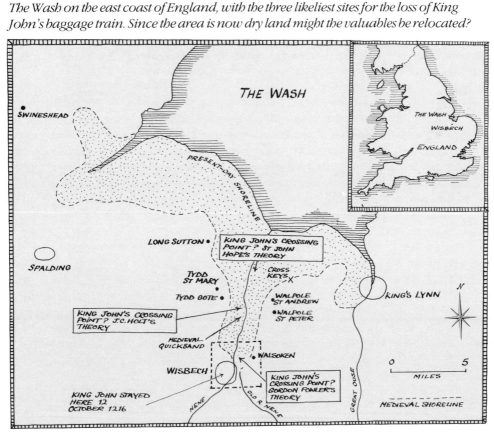

An artist's reconstruction of the moment of disaster for King John as his valuables are swept away. But exactly where and how did the incident happen?

But possibly the most accurate version of the story is that of Abbot Ralph of Coggeshall's *Chronicon Anglicanum*. A Cistercian who wrote between 1207 and 1218, Ralph may well have heard the story from his fellow monks at Swineshead:

> Moreover, the greatest distress troubled him, because on that journey [from King's Lynn] he had lost his chapel with its relics, and some of his packhorses with divers household effects at the Wellstream, and many members of his household were submerged in the waters of the sea, and sucked into the quicksand there, because they had set out incautiously and hastily before the tide had receded.

One notable feature of these earliest stories is that they identify the scene of the disaster as the Wellstream, and make no mention of the Wash. The simple reason for this would seem to have been that in subsequent centuries the Wellstream completely disappeared from maps as a result of changed topography. Another feature is that instead of, as in popular supposition, King John losing merely some box of jewels, the truth of the story seems to have been that either the whole, or a substantial part of the whole royal baggage train was swept or sucked away in the tragedy. King John died just a week after the accident, and according to some interpretations this was because of his grief at the loss.

Since the discovery of a thirteenth-century royal baggage train, with or without any accompanying precious items, would inevitably be of considerable historical interest, among the key questions to be answered are what exactly was lost, what were the precise circumstances of the accident, and where, so far as can be determined, did it occur. In this context the term 'baggage train', one used by modern investigator Mr St John Hope of the London Society of Antiquaries in a lecture of 1906, may be something of a misnomer. While it implies a cumbersome and slow-moving collection of horse-drawn vehicles, this is rather difficult to reconcile with the actual known itinerary of King John and his entourage during the period in question. According to the Patent and Close Rolls for October 1216, King John's movements, with modern mileages added, were:

2 October 1216	Lincoln to Grimsby	37 miles approx.
4 „ „	Grimsby to Louth	16 „ „
5 „ „	Louth to Boston	31 „ „
6 „ „	Boston to Swineshead	7 „ „
7 „ „	Swineshead to Spalding	14 „ „
9 „ „	Spalding to King's Lynn	33 „ „
12 „ „	King's Lynn to Swineshead	47 „ „

The disaster in fact occurred on the morning of the 12th, making it likely that on the 11th, King John would have travelled the thirteen miles from King's Lynn to as far as the east bank of the Wellstream, there finding that the tide was not suitable for an immediate crossing to Wisbech.

But the point of these mileages, given that October days are relatively short, and three miles per hour is a good average for the likely progress of people and pack animals on unmade roads, is that the royal road show could only have been of a relatively light and highly mobile kind in order to keep up such a cracking pace. Although St John Hope supposed a two-mile-long baggage train, it is most unlikely that it would have been as large or as elaborate as this. St John Hope surmised that King John perhaps travelled independently of his baggage train, and that this was why the king himself was not swept away in the accident. But the entourage would in fact have had to manage the same mileages as King John in order to serve its purpose, and given the uncertainty of the times, it would have been much more secure if kept together. That King John was indeed with the party at the time is strongly indicated by the information in the chronicles that the king 'barely' escaped with his own life.

Such considerations are highly relevant to what happened and where, because while St John Hope postulated the baggage train taking a different route to the king, and being overwhelmed at a point between Cross Keys and Long Sutton (see map), a more recent authority, Gordon Fowler, writing in the *Proceedings of the Cambridge Antiquarian Society* in 1952, argued that both were caught up in the same incident at the point where the king is known to have crossed the Wellstream, just by Wisbech. Since the two locations are six and a half miles apart, it is hard to see how the king could have 'barely' escaped with his life if the disaster had occurred at Cross Keys-Long Sutton, so there is a great deal of sense to Gordon Fowler's view.

The tantalizing feature of any would-be search for King John's valuables is that because in more recent centuries there has been extensive land reclamation and diversion of the old waterways that flowed into the Wash, both the Cross Keys and the Wisbech locations are today dry land, with anything that might remain from the accident of 1216 somewhere beneath the soil. In the wake of St John Hope's arguments, most modern endeavours to find King John's baggage train have been focused around Sutton Bridge. In 1929 a licence was granted for a search to be conducted at at 420-acre site called Wingland. Less than a year later a further licence was granted in respect of the 1,100-acre Sutton Bridge Estate. The most massive effort came in 1932 when, financed by a rich American, a company called Fen Research Limited searched 5,470 acres near Sutton Grange. But by 1936 lack of success caused those involved to quarrel between themselves, and the company was ultimately forced into liquidation with debts in excess of £25,000.

So from this point of view alone Gordon Fowler's arguments for the Wisbech location have the greater cogency, raising the question of where in the town's vicinity the original bed of the long defunct Wellstream might lie, and where back in 1216 would have been the crossing point for the old road that King John took. As argued by Fowler, from historical sources and on-the-spot observation the old course of the Wellstream can be traced as having run between Wisbech and the tiny village of Walsoken, both mentioned in the Domesday book. According to Fowler:

> The very fact that those two places are so close together and with the Wellstream between them suggests that they came into being each side of an important ford. The Wellstream ran close to the bank at Walsoken and can be traced in the soil even today. It appears to have had an unchanging course there not more than 40 yards wide, and is marked approximately by the county boundary. The present Locomotive Inn, on the north side of that part of the Lynn road that lies between Wisbech and Walsoken, stands on this long extinct, first silted up and later filled-in channel. The line of the supposed ford and the quarter-mile causeway across the one-time salt-marshes west of it, as far as the recently destroyed Mount Pleasant portion of the old seabank, is probably marked by the course of that road. Therefore it seems that it must have been here, opposite the Locomotive Inn, where the present road crosses the extinct channel of the Wellstream, that the accident occurred.

Fowler has even pin-pointed the likely cause of the accident. In the Wash region there is a rare but noted local phenomenon called 'stolen tides', in which tides can sometimes occur as much as two hours earlier than local knowledge would expect, accompanied by a particularly fierce 'eagre', or tidal bore featuring steep, fast-moving waves. A graphic description of one such occurrence was noted by the diarist Ralph Thoresby back in 1680:

> This morning, before we left Wisbech, I had the sight of an Hygre or Eagre, a most terrible flush of water that came up the river with so much violence that it sunk a coal vessel in the town, and with such a terrible noise that all the dogs in it did snarl and bite at the rolling waves, as though they would swallow up the river; the sight of which, having never seen the like before, much affected me, each wave surmounted the other with extraordinary violence.

Was it such an 'eagre' which swept away King John's baggage train? According to one climatologist, Charles Brooks, in his *Climate Through the Ages*, unusual solar activity was responsible for some freak North Sea weather conditions in the early thirteenth century. On 12 October 1216 the normal low water, according to reliable calculations, would have been about noon, and the very highest spring tide was only two days away. As surmised by Fowler, King John would most likely have been

King John's retinue might have been overcome by a sudden 'eagre', or tidal bore, such as this one photographed at Morton in Lincolnshire.

advised that around 10 am was the best time for his retinue to begin fording the Wellstream, and had they done so, and been overtaken by an 'eagre', the result could only have been just what the early chroniclers described. Those unable to reach safety would have been swept upstream towards the point where the old Wellstream began to take a south-westerly direction. So if Fowler is right in this, an area occupied today by modern housing estates would be the likeliest spot for any would-be searchers to begin digging.

But since Fowler wrote this article an alternative reconstruction has been proposed by a Mr J. C. Holt, writing in the journal *Nottingham Medieval Studies* in 1961. According to Holt, Wisbech was not on the normal route across the fens during the thirteenth century. Furthermore, as he has pointed out, since Fowler wrote his article there has been found evidence of wet quicksand at medieval levels in the area of the old estuary of the Wellstream a few miles north of Wisbech, near the possible line of a natural causeway by which the river was normally crossed. Agreeing with Fowler that King John would have travelled with his baggage train – 'in an area like the Fenland which was predominantly rebel in sympathy and where travel by road was difficult, there would be powerful reasons for keeping an undivided column. . . . The king especially, was unlikely to let such of his regalia, money and precious movables as he had with him, far from his sight.' – Holt has identified the likeliest spot for the disaster as between Walpole and Tydd Gote, i.e. neither as far north as contended by St John Hope, nor as far south as argued by Gordon Fowler.

According to J. C. Holt, this area between Walpole and Tydd Gote may have been the scene of King John's baggage train disaster. As indicated by the faint lines of former creeks, the present-day river Nene almost certainly follows the course of the old Wellstream at this point.

The one objection to Holt's argument is that whatever the normal route might have been, King John indisputably spent part of the disastrous 12 October at Wisbech. However, Holt has a plausible explanation for this. He suggests that because of their losses in the disaster, King John and his army were obliged to make a hasty detour to Wisbech so that salvaged baggage retrieved from drowned pack-horses could be sent on by sea to Grimsby, their main destination. In support of this the Patent Rolls, the official state records of the time, show that at Wisbech King John did indeed engage eight shipmen and their vessels to transport his 'goods and merchandise' on to Grimsby.

While a subsequent writer, W.L. Warren, has been doubtful of this particular explanation of the hiring of the ships, the discovery of the medieval quicksands does lend credence to at least the location proposed by Holt. Furthermore, there is justification for belief that King John lost substantially more in the way of royal treasures than envisaged by Fowler. As observed by Warren:

> Between May 1215 and March 1216 John gathered in a great quantity of his jewels, ornamental plate, and regalia from safe-deposit in monastic houses. This property is minutely inventoried in the Patent Rolls and includes dozens

of gold and silver goblets, flagons, basins, candelabra, phylacteries, pendants and jewel-encrusted belts, the coronation regalia and the regalia his grandmother had worn as Empress of Germany – the great crown, purple robes, the golden wand with a dove, the sword of Tristram. Wendover tells us that in the accident at the Wellstream John lost 'the treasures, precious vessels, and all the other things which he cherished with special care', and if we consult the inventory of the regalia gathered together for the coronation of Henry III in 1220 we find that very little of it tallies with what John is known to have possessed four years earlier. The imperial regalia of Empress Matilda are never heard of again.

Warren is careful to qualify this by remarking that it is possible that King John was robbed on his deathbed at Newark the following week. Abbot Ralph of Coggeshall noted that a priest who went to Newark to say a mass for the dead king's soul told him that he had seen men leaving the city laden with loot.

But the likelihood remains, particularly in view of the severe psychological and physical impact the Wellstream disaster appears to have had on the king, that a very substantial amount of precious objects, including royal regalia, was lost in the quicksand, and that if anywhere, the Walpole/Tydd Gote area is the likeliest spot where these are to be found.

So is there any chance that King John's 'treasure' might be relocated and recovered by modern methods? Thankfully, anything that might have survived almost certainly lies buried too deep for casual searchers using metal-detectors. Hopefully therefore, any future search would only be one carried out by a professionally organized and equipped local or national group working according to the best archaeological principles. A fascinating feature of any re-discovery of King John's baggage train is that should it contain royal regalia, these would automatically claim a rightful place among the Crown Jewels of England, and would be of correspondingly priceless historical interest and importance.

SOURCES:

ROGER DE WENDOVER, *Flores Historiarum*, Rolls Series, 84, 2, 195, 196

RALPH OF COGGESHALE, *Chronicon Anglicanum*, Rolls Series, 66, 183, 184

BROOKS, Charles E. P., *Climate Through the Ages*, London, Ernest Benn, 1926

FOWLER, G., 'King John's Treasure', *Proceedings of the Cambridge Antiquarian Society*, 1952, pp. 4-20

HOLT, J. C., 'King John's Disaster in the Wash', *Nottingham Medieval Studies*, 5, 1961, pp. 75-86

JENKINSON, A. V., 'The Jewels Lost in the Wash', *History 8* (1923-4), pp. 163-6

ST JOHN HOPE, W. H., 'The Loss of King John's Baggage Train in the Wellstream in October 1216', *Archaeologia*, Vol. XI, 1906, pp. 93-110

WARREN, W. L., *King John*, London, Eyre Methuen, 1978

THE GOLD OF EL DORADO

In 1532, just forty years after Columbus's first discovery of the Americas, a Spanish force under Francisco Pizarro made an almost unopposed invasion of Peru. They had already succeeded in capturing the Inca leader, Atahuallpa at the city of Caxamalca, when Atahuallpa, already aware of the Spanish greed for gold, decided to try to buy his freedom. As described by the great historian of Pizarro's conquest, William H. Prescott:

. . . he [Atahuallpa] one day told Pizarro that, if he would set him free, he would cover the floor of the apartment on which they stood with gold. Those present listened with an incredulous smile; and, as the Inca received no answer, he said with some emphasis that "he would not merely cover the floor, but would fill the room with gold as high as he could reach"; and,

LEFT: Insatiable in their greed for gold, the Spanish murder the Inca ruler Atahualpa, even after he has lavished the precious metal upon them and accepted Christian baptism. From Guaman Poma's contemporary depictions of Inca life.

FACING PAGE: The site of the fabled El Dorado? The sacred lake Guatavita, into which annual offerings of gold and emeralds were thrown is in Colombia.

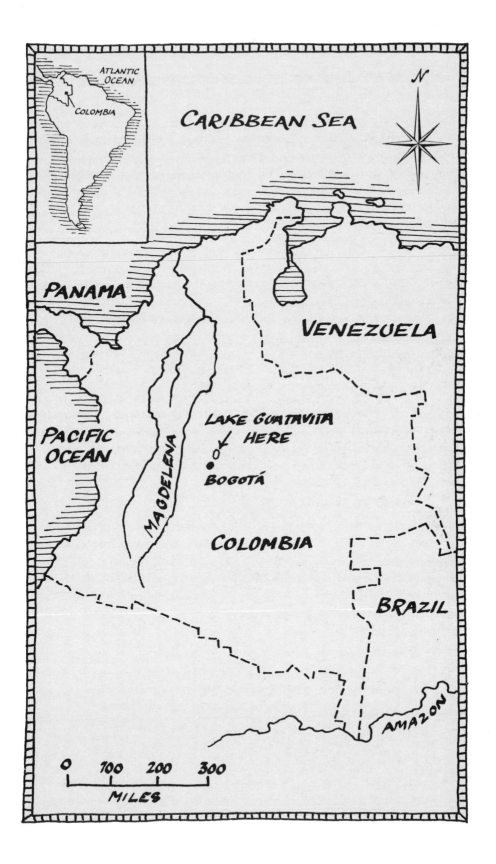

ATLANTIC
OCEAN

COLOMBIA

CARIBBEAN SEA

N

PANAMA

VENEZUELA

PACIFIC
OCEAN

LAKE GUATAVITA
HERE

MAGDELENA

Bogotá

COLOMBIA

BRAZIL

AMAZON

0   100   200   300
MILES

standing on tip-toe, he stretched out his hand against the wall. All stared with amazement; while they regarded it as the insane boast of a man too eager to procure his liberty to weigh the meaning of his words. Yet Pizarro was sorely perplexed. As he had advanced into the country, much that he had seen, and all that he had heard, had confirmed the dazzling reports first received of the riches of Peru. Atahuallpa himself had given him the most glowing picture of the wealth of the capital, where the roofs of the temples were plated with gold, while the walls were hung with tapestry and the floors inlaid with tiles of the same precious metal. There must be some foundation for all this. ... He therefore acquiesced in Atahuallpa's offer, and, drawing a red line along the wall at the height which the Inca had indicated, he caused the terms of the proposal to be duly recorded by the notary. The apartment was about seventeen feet broad, by twenty-two feet long, and the line round the walls was nine feet from the floor. This space was to be filled with gold ... and he demanded two months to accomplish ... this.

Atahuallpa sent orders for all the gold his people could lay their hands on to be brought to Caxamalca, and enormous quantities began arriving, but not in time to satisfy the greed and impatience of the Spanish. Despite the Inca's assurances that he would fully honour his promise, the Spanish garotted him even after he had accepted Christian baptism, and then went on to take the Inca capital, Cuzco, stripping it of every available treasure. In what was effectively an action replay of the earlier conquest of the Aztecs by Cortes, the Inca civilization's most priceless works of art were ruthlessly melted down to be shipped back to Spain in the great plate fleets which plied across the Atlantic in the late sixteenth century.

But despite the enormous quantity of wealth which they found, the Spanish still yearned for more, prompted by stories they had heard of yet more fabulous wealth that was to be found in the mountains beyond the Inca frontiers. When in 1535 one of Pizarro's men, Sebastian Benalcazar, took the city of Quito, he was told about the ruler of a mountainous far-off land who in a special ceremony each year was rowed out in a raft to the centre of a sacred mountain lake. There, divested of all his garments, the king's body was coated in a form of gum, and then sprinkled with gold dust so that he shone like the sun. At the climax of the ceremony this golden man and his people threw emeralds and golden offerings into the lake, the king finally bathing in the lake so that the gold dust in its turn was dissolved away to sink into the deep waters. Thus came into being the story of 'El Dorado' – in Spanish, the Golden One – and Benalcazar was not slow in mounting an expedition to find where this extraordinary ritual took place. Within four years his was but one of three expeditions to make their way deep into what is today Colombia, there founding, not far from the sacred lake, now known as Guatavita, the present-day Colombian capital of Bogotá. But already in 1539 the particular royal dynasty responsible for the ceremony of 'El Dorado' had been overthrown, and all that remained was the story, a lot of gold and emeralds among the local Muisca people ... and the lake.

In by now customary manner the Spanish carried out some ruthless rounds of extermination among the Muisca people in order to try to force the surrender of their treasures. But Lake Guatavita, mist-shrouded, steep-sided, and 9,000 feet above sea level, was to prove far more intractable. In 1545 the soldier Herman Perez de Qesada organized teams of Muisca into bucket gangs in an attempt to drain it.

Lake Guatavita as it looks today. Many unsuccessful attempts have been made to drain it of its treasures.

However, after three months intensive labour the water level had been lowered by only nine feet, enough to reveal some gold objects close to the edge, but clearly only the tiniest fraction of the treasures to be expected in the depths.

In the 1580s it was the turn of a Spanish merchant, Antonio de Sepulveda. He press-ganged 8,000 Muisca to cut a huge channel through the lake's crater-like rim, and when the breach was effected sufficient water poured out to reduce the overall depth by some sixty feet. Again, a considerable quantity of golden ornaments and an emerald the size of a hen's egg were retrieved. But because of the outflow of water there were many landslips, and the hard-won breach became swiftly re-blocked. Furthermore, so many of the Muisca had been killed in all the mishaps that further work had to be abandoned.

For a long while the El Dorado story degenerated into what seemed to many merely an empty legend. In 1596 Sir Walter Raleigh mentioned it in his *Discoverie of Guiana*, but he clearly knew of it only from hearsay. Then in the early 1900s a British company called Contractors Limited decided to make one more attempt to drain Lake Guatavita using a method yet more radical than that of Sepulveda: boring into its mountain cradle so that it could be emptied out from underneath, like the unplugging of a sink. Incredibly, the scheme worked, exposing a lake-bed so thick with soft mud that no-one could walk on it. While the contractors were still thinking how to deal with this problem the mud dried out in the tropical sunshine. However, this only gave rise to a new difficulty. Set like concrete it was now necessary to drill into it for the buried valuables, an eventuality for which the contractors were not prepared. By the time they returned with the right equipment the baked mud had

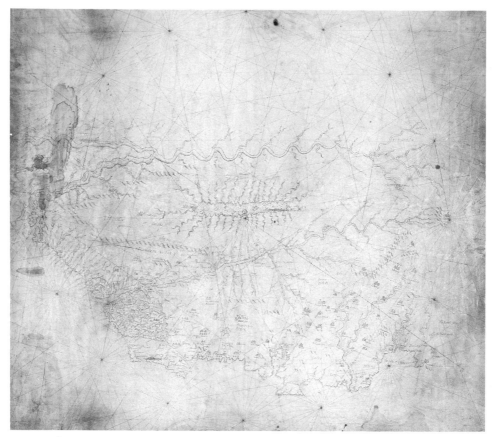

ABOVE: *in his* Discoverie of Guiana *Sir Walter Raleigh imagined El Dorado to be somewhere in the heart of tropical South America.*

FACING PAGE: *gleaming in Bogota's Gold Museum, this Calima (?) gold mask provides an example of the sort of treasures thrown into Lake Guatavita.*

replugged their borehole and tropical rains refilled the lake back to its former level.

Although there have been subsequent attempts, these have similarly been unsuccessful. Now the Colombian government has put a legal protection order on the lake so that any further ventures can be carried out only with the appropriate permissions. To this day no one knows how much gold remains beneath Lake Guatavita's dark waters, but some glimpse is afforded by gold objects that continue to be found from what are almost invariably illegal excavations of ancient graves in Colombia. These include those of the Muisca, and their neighbouring tribes, the Tairona, of the Sierra Nevada mountains, the Pijao of the Magdalena valley, the Sinú of the Caribbean coastal plains, and the Quimbaya of Central Colombia. An exhibition of the ornamental art of these peoples – specifically entitled 'The Gold of El Dorado' was held at the Royal Academy, London in 1979. Sadly, all too little is known of the peoples who made these objects because the Spanish exterminated them so ruthlessly that today only an isolated branch of the Tairona, the Ika, survives in anything like its pre-Conquest form. And these jealously guard their old religion,

Although the Spanish melted down immense quantities of American Indian gold, some examples, such as this Tolima figure, have survived.

and their privacy. According to the explorer and naturalist David Attenborough:
> None today work gold or make marvellous jewels like those worn by their ancestors, the Tairona. But some travellers who visit these mountains regularly say that, every now and then, all the Ika villages empty. The people have gone to some secret valley high in the mountains. As the tribe assembles, sentries are posted along the valleys to warn of the approach of strangers. And when the people are assured that they are at last alone and beyond the reach of the outside world, they begin their most important rituals. The priests appear and dance before the people wearing golden masks and regalia as fine as anything that has been stolen from their ancestors.

What of the story of the Muisca Golden One, the original El Dorado? Besides those gold objects that were recovered from Lake Guatavita, is there anything else to support the tale? In 1969 two farmers, exploring a cave near Bogotá (or at least that is their story), came across a beautifully made nine-inch long specimen of Muisca goldcraft that seems to represent El Dorado himself, erect in elaborate head-dress, and accompanied by eight attendants on board a raft. It is difficult to interpret it as anything other than a portrayal of the lost Muisca ceremony.

So almost certainly Lake Guatavita genuinely does contain a king's ransom of Muisca treasure waiting to be re-discovered. But the Muisca intended it for the god of their sacred lake, and one cannot help feeling that out of respect for the memory of their so-abused ancestors it is there in that lake that it should remain . . .

SOURCES:

PRESCOTT, William H., *History of the Conquest of Peru, with a preliminary view of the Civilization of the Incas*, London, Richard Bentley, 1847 (2 vols.)

ATTENBOROUGH, David, 'The Gold of El Dorado', *Sunday Times Magazine*, November 1979

BRAY, Warwick, *The Gold of El Dorado,* Exhibition catalogue, the Royal Academy, London, 1979

THE BASING HOUSE HOARD

Just to the east of the town of Basingstoke in southern England lies the tiny, brick-cottaged village of Basing, on the banks of the river Loddon. It has a long history. Iron Age pottery and Roman coins have been found during modern excavations. In Saxon times there was a fortress, the Old Castle of Basing, referred to in William the Conqueror's *Domesday Book*, and a Norman New Castle was built on virtually this same spot.

But it was in Tudor times that the site reached the height of its importance with the construction inside the castle earthworks of a magnificent fortified mansion, to become known as Basing House. Standing on rising ground, and surrounded by a

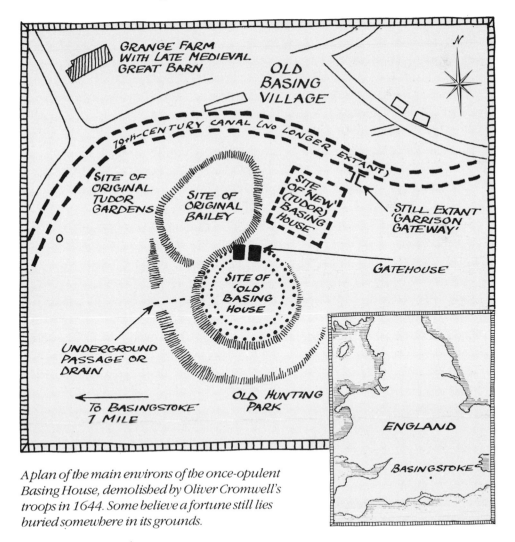

A plan of the main environs of the once-opulent Basing House, demolished by Oliver Cromwell's troops in 1644. Some believe a fortune still lies buried somewhere in its grounds.

ABOVE: An engraving of the one-time appearance of Basing House. Almost all reliable records of this magnificent house have been lost.

FACING PAGE: Sir William Paulet, first Marquis of Winchester, who enriched Basing House from his share in the Dissolution of the Monasteries.

very deep moat, Basing House was erected under the direction of one of the sixteenth-century's most long-lived public figures, Sir William Paulet, first Marquis of Winchester, and household controller and lord chamberlain to Henry VIII, then lord treasurer to Edward VI, and the queens Mary and Elizabeth. Sir William attributed his remarkable political survival during such a troubled era to 'behaving like a willow rather than an oak', and as royal treasurer at the time of the Dissolution of the Monasteries he certainly ensured that his 'poor house' (as it was described on Henry VIII's visit there in October 1535), was one of some splendour. Edward IV and his retinue were entertained there for four days, followed by the court of Mary Tudor and her new husband Philip II of Spain for five days in 1554, followed in 1560 by Elizabeth I, who was so well received that she is said to have remarked: 'By my troth, if my Lord Treasurer were but a younger man I could find it in my heart to have him for a husband before any man in England.' Although at that time Sir William was already about seventy-five years old he survived for another twelve years, his great-grandson, the fourth Marquis, re-entertaining Elizabeth and her court for thirteen days, at great expense, in 1601.

Such royal entertainments proved so expensive that, according to some accounts, part of Basing House had to be taken down to pay for them. But a far worse fate was to be in store for the mansion when, during the 1640s, it became caught up in the

dramatic events of the English Civil War. The then owner was John, fifth Marquis of Winchester, Sir William's great, great-grandson, who took the Royalist side, and was said to have engraved with a diamond the motto 'Aimez Loyauté' (Love Loyalty) on every one of the house's window-panes. In the late summer of 1643 with a force of only 250 men the Marquis successfully held out against a three-month-long attack by the combined Parliamentary troops of Hampshire and Sussex. In July of the following year he twice refused calls for surrender, despite having been wounded by a musketball, and in the September, with the help of a hundred reinforcements, he successfully drove the Parliamentarian besiegers out of Basing.

But to the Marquis's chagrin, by November the Parliamentarians were back, this time with thousands more soldiers and cavalry. Even so, despite severe shortages of food, still he managed to hold out for nearly another year, at one critical stage having his supplies replenished in the nick of time by a Royalist force from Oxford led by Colonel Henry Gage. Nonetheless, outside the walls of Basing hopes of Royalist success were being steadily eroded. Oliver Cromwell won the crucial battle of Naseby, the former Royalist strongholds of Leicester, Bridgwater, Bath, Sherborne and Bristol all surrendered in quick succession, and when Cromwell appeared in person to take charge of the Basing siege, the Royalist cause already seemed irretrievably lost.

Indomitably, the obstinate Marquis still refused to surrender, sending a message to Cromwell that if the King had no more ground in England than Basing House, he would continue to defend it to the last extremity. Now, particularly with many Catholics as well as Royalists known to have sought refuge at Basing, it was a matter of loss of face for Cromwell if he did not manage to snuff out this last pocket of resistance. So four cannon fired in quick succession at 6 am on the morning of 14 October became the signal for an all-out Parliamentarian attack. As described by a contemporary Parliamentarian diarist:

> Our men fell on with resolution and cheerfulness. Immediately the dreadful battery began the great guns discharged their choleric errand with great execution; many wide breaches were made in an instant and the besieged immediately marshalled themselves and stood like a new wall to defend them; our men in full bodies and with great resolution came on. The dispute was long and sharp. The enemy deserved no quarter and I believe that they had little offered them. You must remember what they were. They were most of them Papists, therefore our muskets and our swords did show but little compassion. With undaunted courage our men got over the works, entered the breaches and possessed part of the New House and the court betwixt that and the Old House. We lost but one man before got within their works but took the New House after hot dispute . . .

Despite a spirited last stand at the New House, during which many Parliamentarians were killed when the defenders fired and bombed the intervening bridge, further resistance was effectively hopeless. Amid scenes of terrible destruction of his ancestral home, the Marquis was captured, stripped of everything he possessed, and led away into captivity.

In the hours that followed the Parliamentarian forces were given free rein to pillage most of what they could lay their hands on. As inventoried, the haul included 10 cannon, 600 muskets and assorted swords, numerous horses and sets of troop-

'The Storming of Basing House', from a nineteenth-century painting by C. W. Cope in the Peers' Corridor of the House of Lords

ers' armour, 300 flitches of bacon, 200 barrels of salt beef, 4,000 pounds of cheese, and some £200,000 worth of plate, jewels, furniture, clothing and coin chests, together with many Catholic books, copes, crosses and candlesticks. The buildings and grounds, despite heavy damage during the fighting, clearly would not have disgraced a royal palace. Cromwell's chaplain, Hugh Peter, in his report to the House of Commons, described the whole place as one that 'would have become an emperor to dwell in'. But Cromwell's stormtroopers saw that it did not stay that way:

> In all these great buildings not one iron bar was left in the windows, and by Wednesday morning they had hardly left one lead gutter about the House, and what the soldiers left the fire took hold on which made more than ordinary haste, leaving nothing but bare walls and chimneys in less than twenty hours.

But even with Basing House so badly ravaged, Cromwell, as had been his policy in Bristol, was determined that there should be no opportunity for the place to become a centre of resistance ever again. On 19 October the House of Commons ordered that the mansion be 'totally slighted and demolished', with all its stone, brick and other construction materials free to anyone who wanted to take them away, an enactment obeyed with such enthusiasm that there remained 'scarce one stone left upon another'. When the site was surveyed in 1798, it was found, inclusive of immediate gardens, to encompass some fourteen and a half acres. Today, one of the only portions to have survived is the arched entrance that formed part of the original gatehouse. Of the rest, even original maps and estate papers are no longer extant, and the one-time magnificence of one of the greatest of English castles can only be guessed at from a handful of none-too-informative old engravings.

But the mystery of Basing House is that subsequent to its destruction there has grown up a legend that the defeated Marquis left some £3 million worth of gold somewhere inside, hidden perhaps in foundations that Cromwell's demolition men failed to reach. The possibility of at least some substance to the story was demonstrated at the end of the eighteenth century by the discovery of several gold coins of the appropriate period during the digging of the Basingstoke Canal, which was routed through the House's ruins.

The idea that Civil War treasure may genuinely lie somewhere in the grounds has certainly been taken seriously by a present-day descendant of the fifth Marquis, Mr Christopher Orde-Powlett, whose family continued to own the site up to the twentieth century. In 1963 Mr Orde-Powlett allowed a metal-detector survey to be made in the area of the old chapel, but although this indicated the presence of buried metal, weeks of digging failed to disclose anything more than old musket balls, stained glass and ancient pottery. Similarly, although in 1965 frogmen from the Royal Engineers explored the bottom of the ninety-foot well that had enabled the besieged to hold out for so long during the Civil War, again they found nothing.

Today, the Basing House site is managed by the Hampshire County Council whose officials maintain a neutral opinion on the likelihood of any treasure. One difficulty is the fact that the Marquis did manage to survive his adversity, and therefore had he genuinely hidden a fortune in some secret place he might surely have been expected to return for this. At the time of his capture all his estates were confiscated and he was sent to the Tower of London for high treason. And fifteen years later at the Restoration of Charles II in 1660 he was freed and what remained of his lands were restored to him. Because even by then Basing House was no more than rubble he spent his last years at Englefield, Berkshire, a property he had acquired through his second marriage, but it seems most unlikely that he would not have sought out at Basing any secret cache of money that he thought the Parliamentarians might have missed. He had all the more financial reason for making such a search since, due to the general inefficiency of the time, he never received the £10,000 compensation for his lost estates which Charles II's Parliament awarded him. So it is possible, indeed almost likely, that the quest for the Basing House treasure has been one for a treasure that never was. Even so, it would be most improbable that such a fascinating and historic old mansion has yet yielded up all the secrets of its subterranean recesses.

SOURCES:

PETER, Hugh, *Relation of the Rifling of Basing House*, London, 1645

BAIGENT, F. J., and J. E. Millard, *A History of the Ancient Town and Manor of Basingstoke . . . the siege of Basing House AD. 1643-1645*, C. J. Jacob, Basingstoke, 1889

Dictionary of National Biography, entries for William Paulet, first Marquis of Winchester (c. 1485-1572), John Paulet, fifth Marquis of Winchester (1598-1675), and Inigo Jones

HOLDER, John, and Chris Scott, *The Story of Basing House and a Guide to its Ruins*, Hampshire County Council, 1980

BONNIE PRINCE CHARLIE'S ARMY PAYROLL

When at the death of Elizabeth I of England the Scottish king James VI succeeded to the throne as James I of England, it might have been thought that there and then a satisfactory, all-time union between the two traditionally feuding kingdoms had been made. But this was not to be. The Scottish Stuarts proved unpopular as a dynasty of English kings, James I's son, Charles I losing his head in 1649 at the time of the Civil War, and Charles I's second son, the Catholic James II being deposed during the essentially bloodless Revolution of 1688.

With the English implicated in the Highland massacre of the Macdonald clan at Glencoe in 1692, Highlanders at least were scarcely likely to be enthusiastic about the Act of Union passed fifteen years later by which the forty-five Scottish members and sixteen Scottish peers passed somewhat toothlessly into the London Parliament. Small wonder therefore that it was Highlanders who were principally behind the rebellion in 1715 in support of James II's son, James Francis Stuart, the 'Old

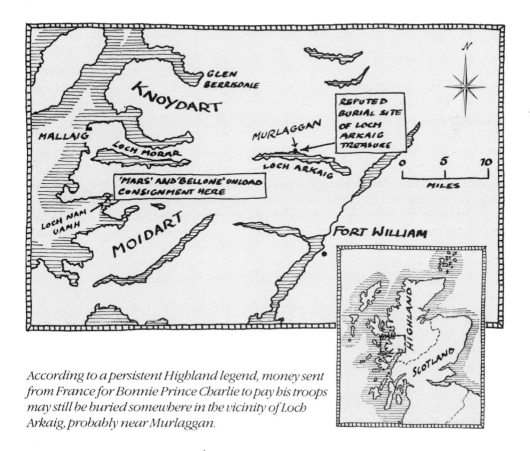

According to a persistent Highland legend, money sent from France for Bonnie Prince Charlie to pay his troops may still be buried somewhere in the vicinity of Loch Arkaig, probably near Murlaggan.

The Battle of Culloden, 16 April 1746, by which Bonnie Prince Charlie's rebellion was hopelessly crushed. The Highlanders' pay is thought to have been sent before news of the disaster reached France.

Pretender'. And it was Highlanders again who, thirty years later, were to rise in support of the Old Pretender's rather more appealing son Charles Edward Stuart, better known to posterity as 'Bonnie Prince Charlie'.

Of course, as history proved, neither rebellion was successful. There were a variety of reasons, but one was certainly not any lack of support from one key quarter, the Stuart's ever-friendly ally, the kingdom of France. It was France, perennially at war with England at that time, who provided a fleet to carry the Old Pretender to the Firth of Forth when he attempted a preliminary landing in his prospective kingdom in 1708. It was by courtesy of French royal hospitality that a suitable place of refuge was provided for both Pretenders during their long years of waiting, planning the right moment to attempt to return to power. And it was French money that lay behind Bonnie Prince Charlie's gallant but ill-supported attempt to overthrow England's Hanoverian monarchy in 1745, an attempt ruthlessly crushed one year later by the Duke of Cumberland's forces at the battle of Culloden just outside Inverness.

This is the background against which must be set perhaps Scotland's greatest 'buried treasure' mystery, that of Bonnie Prince Charlie's army's payroll, lost, according to an oft-quoted legend, somewhere in the vicinity of Loch Arkaig. As the story runs, before news of the Culloden disaster reached France, there had set out from Nantes two French frigates, *La Bellone* and *Le Mars*, loaded with stores, weapons and money to help the rebel cause. Having successfully dodged English patrols, on 10 May 1746 they managed to put in at Loch Nam Uamh off Scotland's western coast where they were met by a number of now fugitive Highlanders, among these the Duke of Perth, Lord John Drummond and Lord Elcho. But even while the two frigates were being unloaded, onto the scene swept two English naval vessels, HMS *Greyhound* and HMS *Terror*, who immediately opened fire. For their own protection the *Mars* and *Bellone* promptly set sail, engaging in a lively action with the English, and leaving all the supplies and money on the water's edge.

The sight of so much brandy and gold there for the picking proved too much for the nearby Macdonald clan of Barisdale, who fell upon the consignment, looting 240 casks of brandy and 800 *louis d'or*. As the news spread, the Macleans of Mull also arrived and took their own share of the pickings. Whatever remained of the consignment, it is said, was secreted eastwards to somewhere in the vicinity of the Murlaggan part of Loch Arkaig. And because the men who buried it were most likely killed during 'butcher' Cumberland's reprisals, arguably it remains there to this day, its exact location unknown.

If the story is indeed true, then it is perhaps one of the assignments in which the responsible amateur 'treasure-hunter' might have a legitimate role to play. So long as the hiding-place is nowhere that would constitute disturbance of a site of historical importance, and so long as all rules are obeyed relating to public and private property (no one wants hundreds of people digging holes in the Highlands), it does at least provide an interesting quarry for the treasure-seeker, one extra and crucial proviso being that expert help should be sought from the very

As envisaged by Victorian romantics, Bonnie Prince Charlie lying exhausted and in hiding after his defeat at Culloden

Loch Arkaig seen from the air. Is Bonnie Prince Charlie's gold still hidden somewhere here?

moment of any find rather than any personal attempt made at excavation. This is because, as in all other such discoveries, any and every detail could be of considerable historical interest, and should be properly recorded and preserved. While any gold found would constitute 'treasure trove', and has by law to be declared, there is now a generous and accepted procedure of rewards for those who carefully follow the rules.

Of course, as in the case of the Basing House treasure, there has to be a substantial risk that the search might be for a treasure that never was. But whether or not there is any 'pot of gold' at the end of the rainbow, the Scottish Highlands does at least provide a not unpleasant terrain in which to look for it.

SOURCES:

McLYNN, F. J. M., *France and the Jacobite Rising of 1745*, Edinburgh, University Press, and New York, Columbia University Press, 1981, pp. 220-221

PREBBLE, John, *Culloden*, London, Penguin, 1970

THE GOLD OF THE ROYAL CHARTER

During the middle of the nineteenth century the *Royal Charter* was a 2,719-ton, 200-hp clipper using both sail and steam for the long voyage between the Australian goldfields and Liverpool in Britain. In October 1859, as the vessel was under sail on the very last stage of its homebound trip, carrying nearly 500 passengers and crew, a registered cargo of £322,400 worth of gold bullion, coin and gold dust, with

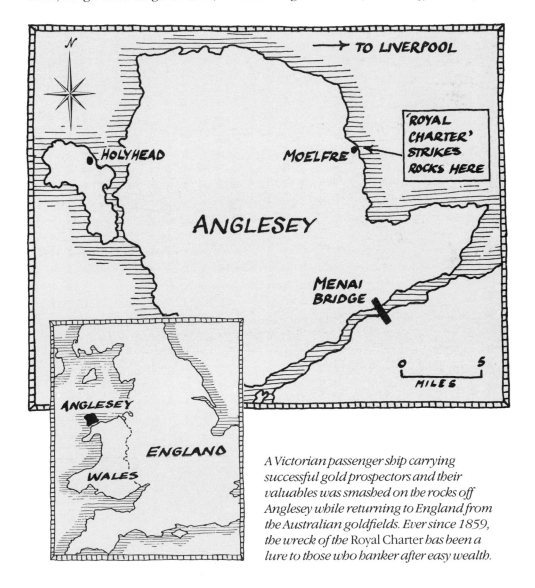

A Victorian passenger ship carrying successful gold prospectors and their valuables was smashed on the rocks off Anglesey while returning to England from the Australian goldfields. Ever since 1859, the wreck of the Royal Charter *has been a lure to those who hanker after easy wealth.*

probably as much again among the many gold prospectors on board, the wind suddenly switched direction from west to east, freshening to gale force as it did so. Seeing his ship beginning to be forced backwards towards the Anglesey coast, its head still to the wind, Captain Taylor gave immediate orders for full steam power, the reefing in of all sails, and the firing of signal rockets to try to summon a pilot boat. But the gale began to tear the sails to shreds, the single steam engine proved no match for the force of the storm, and even the shooting of the anchors in the bows failed to check the ship's now nightmarish drift towards rocks just off the east coast of Anglesey, within a mile of the Moelfre lighthouse.

Fifty yards from the shore the *Royal Charter* began grinding on rocks in nearly four fathoms of water, and although the masts and sails were immediately cut away, these only became entangled with the propeller, adding to the vessel's helplessness. Anglesey residents, alerted by the distress rockets, hurried to see what they could do to help, only to realize that the sea was too violent for the launching of any lifeboat. By a near superhuman effort a Portuguese seaman, Joseph Rogers, managed to get a line from the ship to the beach to try to winch at least some passengers to safety. But it was too late. Already holed, and tossed yet closer to the shore by one huge wave after another, the *Royal Charter* broke in two, spilling hundreds of its occupants and their belongings into the sea.

Four hundred and fifty-nine lives were lost, most by their bodies being smashed

The harrowing scene as gale force winds smashed the Royal Charter *against rocks near Moelfre with the loss of 459 lives*

against the rocks. As the *Illustrated London News* described the scene after the disaster:

> The ironwork of the vessel was in mere shreds; the woodwork was in chips. The coast and the fields above the cliffs were strewn with fragments of the cargo and of the bedding and clothing. Worse still, the rocks were covered with corpses of men and women frightfully mutilated, and strewn with the sovereigns which the poor creatures had gone so far to seek, and were now torn from them in such a pitiful way.

One living individual for whom the wreck of the *Royal Charter* has had more than a passing interest is Mr William Gundry-Mills, great-nephew of the mine lecturer and gold financier Thomas Trevenen Gundry who was one of the all-too-few survivors, managing to swim safely to shore with his personal fortune secured in an easily portable banker's draft. According to what Mr Gundry-Mills learned of the tragedy from his aunt, one reason why the casualties were so high was because many miners tried to swim ashore loaded down with gold stuffed in their pockets. Another reason, particularly among the women was Victorian modesty:

> Many of the women on board drowned because they were too prudish to take off their clothes, and this hindered them while they tried to swim. But in those days not many people knew how to swim anyway, and a lot died because of that.

With so much gold known to have been on board, and the two halves of the wreck clearly visible just off shore, it was inevitable that enterprising Victorian salvors, both official and unofficial, would endeavour to retrieve what they could. So-called hard-hat diving had already been developed, and during 1859-60 divers employed by the official salvors managed to bring up more than £300,000 worth of the gold that had been in solid form. Like the structural portions of the ship, some of this had been extraordinarily mangled by the force of the sea. As was reported by the famous novelist Charles Dickens in *The Times*:

> So tremendous had the force of the sea been when it broke up the ship, that it had beaten one great ingot of gold deep into a strong and heavy piece of solid ironwork; in which also, several loose sovereigns that the ingot had swept in before it, had been found as firmly embedded as though the iron had been liquid when they had been forced there.

As for the gold dust on board, the bags in which it had been stored had been ripped apart in the turmoil, their contents effectively irretrievably spilled into the sea-bed.

But although such a substantial proportion of the gold on board was recovered, with little doubt more remains. Furthermore, the site of the wreck is easy enough to find, since on the Porth Ynys clifftop near Moelfre on the east coast of Anglesey a commemorative limestone obelisk has been erected at the point nearest to the rocks where the ship foundered. The wreck itself is now too broken to be of significant historical value, so the site must inevitably be somewhat of a magnet for any treasure-hunter trained and equipped for underwater searches, and has certainly not gone undisturbed in the last few decades. In the spring of 1958 the now veteran marine archaeologist Sydney Wignall and his colleague Eric Reynolds swam out to the site, finding it unexpectedly close to the shore. As Wignall subsequently described it:

The Anglesey memorial to those 500 passengers and crew who died in the shipwreck of the Royal Charter *in October 1859*

Within a few yards of our point of entry into the water, we were swimming amongst broken iron ribs and frames, and buckled iron plates, embedded in sand. With curiosity we examined and discarded the odd porthole, stanchion and deck fitting, and it was then that I chanced on a large yellow ingot protruding from the sand, jammed between an iron frame and a huge piece of torn, jagged iron plate. It seemed to be a copper bar, and I struggled to free my wreck souvenir. Reynolds joined me and we struggled away at the metal ingot until we eventually ran out of air. Reynolds was first to surface, leaving me struggling alone. In the end, in desperation, I drew my diving knife and, using its saw edge, sawed into the ingot. The metal was soft and yellow. At that moment I realized that I had found a gold bullion bar.

Completely out of air, I surfaced and told Reynolds the news. In 1958 we had no access to a compressed-air supply for our scuba cylinders on the north

Wales coast; the nearest charging point was the British Oxygen Company in Cheshire, about a hundred miles away by road. Three days later we were back, anxious to dive into the sea and recover our prize. We were to be disappointed – a gale was raging in all its fury. A few days later, when the storm had abated, we returned to the site and swam to the spot where a fortune in salvor's reward awaited us. To our horror, the whole configuration of the wreck appeared to have changed. Where we had seen ribs and plates, there rose a mound of sand; where we had seen sandy areas, we were now confronted by previously hidden twisted ironwork. The wreck of the *Royal Charter* had taken the treasure of 1859 back into her bosom.

In case of any doubts concerning what he had found, Wignall subsequently asked a jeweller to assay the tiny gold specks that he noticed still clinging to the cutting edge of his diving knife. The jeweller confirmed them as 23-carat gold. On Wignall's rough calculations the ingot with which he and Reynolds had struggled must be worth something over £300,000 at today's gold values – if it could be retrieved. But

Fruits of recent salvage work: a gold ring engraved 'Ovens' and a sovereign from the Sydney mint dated 1859

Wignall has never been back to try to relocate it, insisting that he is not a treasure hunter, and in any case prefers to work in warmer climes than the waters off the English and Welsh coasts.

But others have been less easily deterred. In 1972 diver Jack Leyland Smart and other Anglesey locals founded a Royal Charter Salvage Expedition, which in the course of some twelve years of probings with suction and airlifting apparatus established that a very substantial proportion of the original ship is still lying in three broken sections embedded at varying depths in the sea-bed. Then, in the summer of 1985 a Liverpool-based diving-team, Best Speed, arrived at the wreck site, and with typical treasure-hunting destructiveness proceeded to dynamite their way to the more deeply buried portions of the wreck. They brought up sovereigns, a gold nugget, a gold ring and some hundred other items which, in accordance with the law, they handed over to the Official Receiver of Wrecks in expectation that these would be returned to them in due course. But then, having run up debts and ill-will among the Anglesey residents, in mid-November 1985 Best Speed abruptly abandoned their land-based camp, leaving the local Royal Charter Salvage Expedition to resume charge. During 1986 Jack Smart's men worked for months on fresh clearance of sand and silt – only to see their efforts destroyed in a matter of hours by the changes to the sea-bed wrought by Hurricane Charlie which swept across the Irish Sea to hit the Anglesey coast on 25 August.

Tantalizingly close though it lies to the shore, the *Royal Charter* wreck is therefore one which does not seem inclined to give up its contents too easily.

SOURCES:

The Illustrated London News, 5 Nov. 1859

'Shipwrecked gold mine surfaces off Anglesey', *The Times*, 10 July 1985

'Diver's wreck undertaking', *The Times*, 31 July 1985

WIGNALL, Sydney, *In Search of Spanish Treasure: A Diver's Story*, Newton Abbot, Devon, David & Charles 1982, pp. 13-16.

Correspondence with Sydney Wignall and Jack Leyland Smart

THE GOLD OF CUSTER'S
LAST STAND

One of the most famous stories in the history of the United States is that of General Custer and the over-whelming of his five companies of the Seventh Cavalry by an unprecedented massing of Sioux and Cheyenne Indians in the valley of the Little Big Horn River, south-ern Montana, on 25 June 1876. Since there were no white survivors of the final incident, one of the few sources of information about what happened derived from Indians such as the Cheyenne chief 'Two Moon', who gave the following account to a newspaper reporter in 1898:

The Sioux rode up the ridge on all sides, riding very fast. The Cheyennes went up the left way. Then the shooting was quick, quick. Pop-pop-pop very fast. Some of the soldiers were down on their knees, some standing. Officers all in front. The smoke was like a great cloud, and everywhere the Sioux went, the dust rose like smoke. We circled round them – swirling like water round a

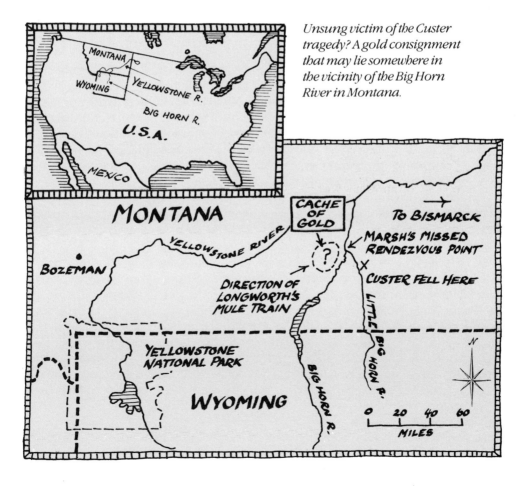

Unsung victim of the Custer tragedy? A gold consignment that may lie somewhere in the vicinity of the Big Horn River in Montana.

stone. Soldiers drop and horses fall on them. Soldiers in line drop, but one man rides up and down the line – all the time shouting. He rode a sorrel horse with white face and white forelegs, I don't know who he was. He was a brave man. . . . Once in a while some man would break out and run toward the river but he would fall. . . . All along the bugler kept blowing his commands. He was very brave too. Then a chief was killed. I hear it was Long Hair [the Sioux name for Custer]; and then a bunch of men, may be so forty, started toward the river. The man on the sorrel horse [probably Custer's Chief of Scouts] led them, shouting all the time. He wore a buckskin short, and had long black hair and mustache. He fought hard with a big knife. His men were all covered with white dust. . . . One man all along ran far down toward the river, then round up over the hill. I thought he was going to escape but a Sioux fired and hit him in the head. He was the last man.

When all was over Custer, fourteen officers and 233 of his men lay dead, their bodies stripped and savagely mutilated according to Indian custom. But if it was a sad loss of manpower, it was a far greater loss for American pride. Legend has it that the Sioux chief Sitting Bull, who remained aloof from the actual attack, commented when he heard the news: 'Now they will never leave us alone'. And he was right. Although it might have been Custer's Last Stand, it was also the last really serious incidence of Sioux resistance.

Inevitably, the story of the disaster swept America from coast to coast, and the subsequent debates over whether Custer was an hero or an incompetent filled newspaper columns for months, if not years to follow. As a result, almost completely overlooked was the story of the loss of a substantial shipment of gold buried for safety amid the very same amassing of Indians in which Custer met his end.

For just the day before Custer's last battle, when the General was in hot pursuit of Indians that he had heard to be in the vicinity of Montana's Big Horn and Little Big Horn rivers, a supply boat called the *Far West* was making a difficult upstream journey to the junction of the same rivers for a pre-arranged rendezvous with Custer's commanding officer, General Alfred H. Terry. At about the same time, some fifty miles to the west, a mule-drawn freight wagon from Bozeman, Montana, with miner's gold worth some £30,000 at 1876 prices, was making its way towards Bismarck, North Dakota, its driver Gil Longworth and his two armed guards becoming increasingly worried by their repeated narrow escapes from hostile groups of Indians.

By 26 June, the day after the Custer massacre, Captain Marsh of the supply boat, who had never previously navigated so far up the Big Horn, discovered that he had missed the rendezvous point, and had travelled some fifteen to twenty miles too far up-stream. While he was anchored in the early evening intending to return down-stream the next day, an exhausted and badly frightened Longworth with the freight-waggon met up with him. Pouring out a terrifying tale of how the whole area was swarming with hostile Indians, Longworth pleaded with Marsh to take over the shipment of gold and deliver it to Bismarck when he could, as he seriously doubted his own chances of getting through alive. Marsh agreed, and took the gold on board, whereupon a relieved Longworth with his two guards returned west back towards Bozeman, Montana.

But when at dusk numerous columns of Indian camp fires became visible all

ABOVE: Custer's Battle of the Little Big Horn, 25 June 1876, from an imaginative lithograph by Kurz and Allison. The battlefield is now a United States National Monument, and recent ballistics and forensic studies of bullets and human bones found there indicate that the Indian success was almost certainly due to their earlier capture of newly developed repeating rifles, superior to anything that had been issued to Custer's cavalry. These enabled the Indians to out-gun Custer's men two to one, after which they finished them off in hand-to-hand fighting with clubs and axes.

RIGHT: Major-General George A. Custer, whom the Indians knew as 'Long Hair', from a photograph by Brady. He was killed alongside his men, almost certainly on what is today known as Last Stand Hill.

round, Marsh realized that Longworth had not exaggerated the dangers. Deciding that the only prudent course lay in hiding the gold at some suitable spot on shore, then returning for it when the Indian unrest had subsided, he ordered his deck-hands to row it ashore in two boats, then, aided by his two most trusted officers, first mate Ben Thompson and Foulk his engineer, he set about the task of arranging a suitable place of concealment. Although exactly what the three men did is unrecorded, they were back on board within three and a half hours.

During the next forty-eight hours, in which Marsh made contact with General Terry's main army, the full horror of the Indian onslaught became known. Custer's men had not been the only ones to be caught out. A force under Major Reno only barely escaped the same fate, suffering many casualties whom Marsh was immediately detailed to ship down-river for treatment in Bismarck. As for Gil Longworth and his companions, the bodies of the two guards were found along with the burned-out wagon at Pryor's Creek, and Longworth himself, riddled with bullets, some way further on at Clark's Fork.

Because of the continued danger from Indians, it was another three years before Marsh managed to get to Bozeman, Montana, attempting at that time to trace the freight company for whom Longworth had been working. But he discovered that, precisely because so many gold shipments had been attacked by Indians, the company had gone out of business, and with it all record of the various prospectors

A Crow encampment on the Little Big Horn River, from a photograph taken by a Montana photographer, Richard Throssel in 1908. Does the ill-fated Gil Longworth's gold consignment still lie buried somewhere along this river?

who had originally mined the gold.

And so far as can be determined, Marsh thereupon made no attempt to retrieve the cache, continuing to make an honest living as a river-boat captain up to his retirement at the age of seventy-two, and never throughout his life showing any sign of having struck sudden wealth. The same appears to have been true of his two helpers in the concealment of the cache, first mate Thompson and engineer Foulk, both of whom continued working, Thompson still as first mate on the *Far West* when she was sold to new owners in Missouri, and Foulk with him up until his retirement through ill-health in 1892. As in the case of Marsh, neither man's subsequent life shows the slightest sign of having struck it rich.

Accordingly, since Marsh, Thompson and Foulk were the only three individuals to know where they hid the gold, there has to be a strong likelihood that the cache is most likely still where they left it, if only it could be relocated. Certainly this is the opinion of one American writer, Emile C. Schurmacher, who came across the story quite accidentally while researching the operations of General Terry at the time of the Custer massacre. The main available clues are that the spot was fifteen to twenty miles up the Big Horn River from the mouth of the Little Big Horn, and most likely on the west bank, since that was the direction from which Longworth and his companions had come. In view of the fact that it was late evening, and that the whole reason for the concealment was hostile Indians close by, it is very unlikely that Marsh and his helpers strayed far from the river-bank, or that they did much digging, since fresh earth would readily have been spotted. In any case, they returned to the boat within three and a half hours.

So if the gold is still there, the most likely method of rediscovering it would be first to determine along the appropriate stretch of river the various locations Marsh might most readily have chosen for anchorage in the particular circumstances of June 1876, then to try to think out what natural place of concealment he might have selected in order to be able to return to the safety of the boat at the earliest possible moment. Schurmacher is known to have already made at least one unsuccessful expedition, but possibly he was wrong to assume the cache to have been on the west bank, besides which he may not have allowed sufficiently for any discrepancy in Marsh's estimate of having been fifteen to twenty miles too far up-stream.

A cache of gold worth a fortune at today's values could be awaiting a determined researcher with the patience and resources to explore the likely area in depth. This is a happy example of a quest that should be open to anyone, without the requirements of any special expertise. For although anyone finding the cache should obviously take care not to destroy anything, most particularly the wrappings and labels accompanying the gold, the cache's prime value would be its intrinsic one, i.e. the gold itself. As in the case of the Bonnie Prince Charlie gold, the responsible searcher should proceed only after having obtained appropriate permissions from relevant local landowners. But with Custer's last stand now well over a century ago, at least there should be little danger from marauding Indians.

SOURCES:

RAWLING, G. S., 'Custer's Last Stand', *History Today*, January 1962, pp. 57-66

NORVILL, Roy, *The Treasure Seeker's Treasury*, London, Hutchinson, 1978, pp. 61-68

A CHRONOLOGY
OF THE
DISCOVERED

By no means exhaustive, this list simply conveys some of the more major discoveries since the early nineteenth century.

1820 The Venus of Milo discovered in underground chamber by local peasant on the Greek island of Melos

1839 Commencement of uncovering of ancient Mayan city of Copán, Honduras (Belize) by American lawyer John Lloyd Stephens

1843 Commencement of excavations of Assyrian palace of Nineveh by French-born consular official Paul Émile Botta

1845 Commencement of excavations of Assyrian capital Nimrud by British laywer Austin Henry Layard

1854 Mound that represents the site of ancient Ur identified (from inscriptions) by British consul J. E. Taylor

1860 Ancient Khmer city of Angkor Thom discovered deep in Cambodian jungle by French naturalist Henri Mouhot

1873 'Treasure of Priam' discovered by German businessman Heinrich Schliemann on Turkish mound Hisarlik, identified by him as the site of ancient Troy

1876 First grave from presumed Homeric period opened by Heinrich Schliemann at Mycenae

1881 Cache of mummies of Egypt's pharaohs – including Ahmose, Amenophis I, Tuthmosis I, II and III, Seti I and Ramesses II discovered just outside ancient Thebes by Emil Brugsch

1889 Looted tomb of 12th Dynasty pharaoh Amenemhet III discovered in previously unidentified brick pyramid by British archaeologist Sir W. M. Flinders Petrie

1898 Second cache of mummies of Egypt's pharaohs, including Merneptah (claimed by some to have been pharoah of the Exodus), discovered by French archaeologist Victor Loret

1899 Commencement of unearthing of site of ancient Babylon by German archaeologist Robert Koldewey

1900   Commencement of unearthing of Minoan city of Knossos by British scholar Sir Arthur Evans

1900   Ancient wreck filled with Greek bronze and marble statuary dating from 4th century BC discovered by Greek sponge-divers off Andikythera, between the western tip of Crete and mainland Greece

1901   Site of ancient Minoan town located by American archaeologist Harriet Boyd at Gournia in eastern Crete

1903   Norwegian workmen digging into mound 40 miles south of Oslo uncover first indications of Oseberg Viking ship burial

1904   Mayan treasures from sacred well of sacrifice at Chichén-Itzá in the Yucatán, Mexico brought back to the surface by American adventurer-archaeologist Edward Herbert Thompson

1910   So-called Antioch Chalice, part of a cache of early Christian valuables, discovered by Arab workmen digging a well near Antioch in Syria

1911   Inca mountain stronghold of Machu Picchu discovered by American archaeologist Hiram Bingham

1920   Commencement of unearthing of site of Harappa, a major city of the ancient Indus civilization of India, under the direction of Daya Ram Sahni of the Archaeological Survey of India

1922   Site of Indus valley civilization city of Mohenjo-daro identified in Sind by R. D. Banerji of Archaeological Survey of India, and excavation commenced

1922   The tomb of Tutankhamun located and opened by British archaeologist Howard Carter in the Valley of the Kings, Luxor, Egypt

1927   Royal graves uncovered by Englishman Leonard Woolley on the site of ancient Ur

1933   Site of ancient Babylonian city of Mari located by French archaeologist Professor André Parrot at Tell Hariri, on the Euphrates between Damascus and Mosul. Excavations begun

1937   Site of Ezion-geber, naval base of biblical king Solomon located by American archaeologist Nelson Glueck at Tell el-Kheleifeh, near the present-day Israeli resort of Eilat

1939   Discovery of ship burial of 7th century king of East Anglia at Sutton Hoo, near Woodbridge, Suffolk. Full excavation subsequently carried out 1967

1940   Schoolboys exploring at Montignac, France, discover bramble-covered hole in the ground that leads to Lascaux cave paintings dating *c.* 14,000 BC

1940   The Mildenhall treasure, 34 richly decorated pieces of 4th century AD Roman tableware uncovered during ploughing by British farm labourer at West Row, near Mildenhall, Suffolk

1947   Discovery by Bedouin goatherds of the first manuscripts of the so-called
         Dead Sea Scrolls

1953   Discovery beneath the basilica of St Peter's, Rome of a box of bones
         subsequently identified by epigraphist Dr Margherita Guarducci as those of
         the apostle Peter, disciple of Jesus, and first Pope

1954   Previously unknown step pyramid discovered and unearthed by Egyptian
         archaeologist Zakaria Goneim near Saqqara, Egypt

1956   Wreck of the Swedish warship *Wasa*, which sank in the middle of
         Stockholm harbour on her maiden voyage in 1628, relocated by Swedish
         amateur marine archaeologist Anders Franzén, and recovery plans
         commenced

1958   Hoard of late Celtic silver, probably hidden during Viking invasions,
         discovered by local schoolboy during excavation of the foundations of a
         medieval church on St Ninian's Isle in the Shetlands

1961   Minoan palace and port located near Kato Zakro, on eastern coast of Crete,
         by Greek archaeologist Dr Nicholas Platon, and excavation commenced

1961   Wreck of vessel carrying Etruscan and Greek wares discovered by British
         sub-aqua instructor Reg Vallintine off the Mediterranean island of Giglio, on
         the western coast of Italy to the north of Rome

1964   American expedition discovers Vilcabamba, last stronghold of the Incas

1966   Wreck subsequently identified as that of the Henry VIII warship *Mary Rose*
         located off Southsea in the Solent, southern England by British naval
         historian Alexander McKee and American sonar specialist Professor Harold
         Edgerton

1967   Wreck of Spanish Armada galleon *Girona*, sunk laden with rescued crew-
         members from previous Armada shipwrecks, located by Belgian
         underwater treasure-hunter Robert Sténuit at Port na Spaniagh, an inlet a
         few miles north of the mouth of the River Bush in County Antrim, Northern
         Ireland. Recovery of objects of historical interest commenced

1967   Minoan port overwhelmed by volcanic eruption *c.*1500 BC located by Greek
         archaeologist Spiros Marinatos at Akrotiri, on the Aegean island of Thera,
         and excavation commenced

1968   Spanish Armada wreck *Santa Maria de la Rosa* discovered by marine
         archaeologist Sydney Wignall in Blasket Sound off south-west Ireland

1968   From deciphered inscription, mound of Tel Mardikh in north-west Syria
         identified as the site of Early Bronze Age city of Ebla

1970   *El Gran Grifón*, flagship of the Spanish Armada, located by Colin Martin and
         Sydney Wignall in south-east corner of Fair Isle, between Orkney and
         Shetland in Scotland

1971   Wreck of Dutch East Indiaman, the *Lastdrager*, sunk laden with bullion in 1653, located by Belgian Robert Sténuit off Crussa Ness Point on the Shetland island of Yell

1971   Wreck of Spanish Armada merchantman *La Trinidad Valencera* located by City of Derry Sub Aqua Club at western end of Kinnagoe Bay, North Donegal, Ireland

1971   Wrecks of two Spanish galleons, the *Nuestra Senora de Atocha* and *La Margarita*, located 40 miles west of Key West, Florida, by American treasure hunter Mel Fisher

1972   Ancient Greek Bronze statues of warriors discovered off Riace, southern Italy by Italian scuba diver Stefano Mariottini

1974   First statues from terracotta 'army' guarding the tomb of first Chinese emperor Qin Shi Huang Di unearthed by Chinese farm workers at Mount Li, 40 miles from ancient Chinese capital of Xi'an.

1977   Intact tomb of Philip II, father of Alexander the Great discovered by Greek archaeologist Professor Manolis Andronikos at Vergina in northern Greece

1978   Wreck of the *Concepción*, a vessel of the Mexican silver fleet sunk in 1641, relocated on the Silver Bank coral reef, 80 miles north of the Dominican Republic, by American treasure-hunter Burt Webber, and recovery of cargo commenced

1979   Cache of 83 pieces of late Roman gold and silver discovered on a building site in Thetford, Norfolk, by British metal-detector enthusiast, the late Arthur Brooks. Valuable data lost on circumstances in which hoard had originally been hidden

1980   Bullion from wreck of the *Admiral Nakhimoff*, a Russian battle-cruiser sunk in 1904, recovered from Straits of Tushima, south-west of Japan, by expedition financed by Japanese millionaire

1980   Outstanding medieval silver chalice located and clumsily unearthed by Irish treasure-hunters Michael Webb and son at Derrynaflan Church, Tippcrary, Ireland, necessitating months of delicate restoration

1981   £45-million worth of gold bullion from the wreck of the Second World War ship HMS *Edinburgh* successfully located and raised from 800 feet beneath the sea in freezing waters off the coast of the Soviet Union, north of Murmansk

1982   Wreck of the *Lusitania*, sunk by a German submarine in 1915, located 11.8 miles south-west of the Head of Kinsale, Ireland, by British engineer John Pierce and Australian engineer Barry Lister. Recovery of salvageable items commenced

1983   Tomb of the 2nd century BC Chinese emperor Wen Di discovered by Chinese archaeologists at the hill of Xianggan, north of Guangzhou (Canton)

1984   The world's oldest known shipwreck, a vessel of the 15th century BC laden with goods from Greece, Cyprus, and Phoenicia, discovered off Kas, on the south-western coast of Turkey, east of Rhodes

1985   Wreck of the Dutch merchant vessel *Geldermalsen*, sunk on a reef in 1752 laden with tea, gold and 150,000 pieces of Nanking porcelain, located by professional salvor Captain Michael Hatcher, and recovery of cargo commenced

1985   Site of 1,000-year-old lost city of the Chachas people discovered in the Peruvian Andes by American explorer Gene Savoy

1985   Huge cargo of silver bars and coins, estimated value $200 million (£143 million), recovered from *Atocha* wreck by American treasure-hunter Mel Fisher

1985   Wreck of the liner *Titanic* located by joint American-French expedition led by Dr Robert Ballard of the Woods Hole Oceanographic Institute, Massachusetts

1986   Tomb of Maya, treasurer to pharaoh Tutankhamun, located at Saqqara, Egypt by British archaeologist Dr Geoffrey Martin and Dutch colleague Dr Jacobus van Rijk

Index

Page numbers in *italics* refer to illustrations and maps when they are separated from text of a subject.

Absalom's tomb *144*, 149-50
Achor, Vale of *144*, 147-8
Akrotiri, Thera *22*, 24-6
Alaise 33
Albright, Professor William 19
Alcock, Professor Leslie 77
Alesia 30-35
Alexander the Great 60, *62*; tomb 50, 53-4
Alise-Sainte-Reine 32-3, *34*, 35
Allegro, J.M. 147-50
Anglesey: *Royal Charter* 175-80
Anglo-Saxon Chronicle: Badon 47
Angra Bay, Azores *120*, 122
Annales Cambriae 42, 44, 73
Antiochus I, of Commagene 60-63
Antiquities discovered, 1820-1986: list 186-90
Aramburu, Admiral Marcos de 121
Army payroll: loss 171-4
Arthur, King: grave 73-9; Mount Badon 41-5
Ashe, Geoffrey 42, 79
Aspronisi *22*, 24
Astérix and Obélix 30, 33
Atahuallpa (Inca) 158-60
Atlantis 21-6
Attenborough, David: El Dorado 164
Attila the Hun 69-72
Augustus, Emperor 53
Avalon 74, 76, 77, 79
Azores: *Revenge* 120, 121-4

Bab ed-Dra 10
Badbury Rings, Dorset 42
Badon, Mount 41-5
Baker, Professor H. Wright 146
Ballard, Dr Robert 190
Barfleur: *White Ship* 108-11
Basing House hoard 165-70
Bath: Mount Badon *41*, 43-5
Bazán, General Don Alonzo de 121
Beattie, Professor Owen 96
Bedouins: Dead Sea Scrolls 144
Beechey Island: grave *95*
Bellone 171, 172-3
Benaki, Alexander 105-7
Benalcazar, Sebastian 160
Bennett, Annette 42-5
Bertandone, Martin de 121-2
Berthier, André 33-5
Best Speed (diving team) 180
Bible: Herod the Great 64-8; Sodom and Gomorrah 16-20
Big Horn River *181*, 182, 185
Bogotá: El Dorado *158*, 160, *163*, 164
Bonhomme Richard 131-5
Bonnie Prince Charlie: army payroll 171-4
Brown, Frank E. 39
Burkitt, Timothy 42-5

Cacafuego 126
California: Drake 126
Calvert, Frank 138, 143
Camden, William 76, 77
Camelot 78
Camlan 73-4
Cape Artemision: wreck *104*, 105-7
Capitana 115-8
Caracol Bay: *Santa María 112*, 114-5
Carter, Bertam 129-30

Carter, Howard, and Lord Carnarvon *Title page*, 48
Caxamalca: El Dorado 158-60
Chénevée, Dr Henri 28
Christopher 125, 126
Christopher II 125, 126
Cities of the Plain 16-20
Clements, Francis 93-4
Colomb, Georges 33
Colombo: El Dorado *158*, 160-4
Columbus, Christopher 91, 112-19
Commonwealth (freighter) 135
Cossa: Vesuvius 36, *37*, 40
Crete: Atlantis 23-4
Cromwell, Oliver: Basing House 168-70
Cross, 'Arthurian' 76-8
Cross Keys *151*, 153-4
Culloden, and Duke of Cumberland 172-3
Cumberland, George, 3rd Earl 121
Cussler, Clive 135
Custer's last stand: gold 181-5; Custer *181*, 182, *183*
Cuzco (Inca capital) 160

Davis, Theodore 48
Dead Sea: cities 16-20
Dead Sea Scrolls 144-50
Decca Recorder 133-5
Deiss, Joseph Jay 39
Delacroix, Alphonse 33
Demangel, R. 28
Deptford: *Golden Hind 127*, 128-9, 130
Dickens, Charles: *Royal Charter* 177
Diodorus Siculus 19-20
Discovered antiquities, 1820-1986: list 186-90

Discovery (Hudson's ship) 92-6
Divers and diving 9, 20, *91*, 106-7,
   177, 178-80; sonar 9, 117, *118, 119*
Doerner, Dr Friedrich 63
Domesday Book: Basing House 165;
   King John's treasure 154
Donnelly, Ignatius 21-3
Doughty, Thomas 125-6
Doumas, Christos 25-6
Drake, Sir Francis: coffin 86-91:
   Golden Hind 125-30; *Revenge* 120
Drake's Island, Portobelo 86, *89*
Duck Jing, Emperor *57*
Dupont-Sommer, A. 147

Edgerton, Dr Harold 9, 117, *118, 119*
Edinburgh (ship) 9, 189
Edward I: King Arthur 78
Egyptian tombs 47-54
Elbeuf, Prince of 38
El Dorado 158-64
Elizabeth I: *Golden Hind* 128-9
Elizabeth (ship) 91, 125, 126
Emery, Professor W. B. 52
Eratosthenes 28
Essenes (brotherhood) 147, 148
Euboea: wreck *104*, 105-7

Far West 182-4, 185
Fengxiang: tomb 57
Fiorelli, Giuseppe 38
Fitz-Stephen, Ralph 76
Flamborough Head: wreck 132-5
Flemming, Dr Nicholas 29
Flodden 80
Flores, Azores *120*, 121
Fouk (ship's engineer) 184, 185
Fowler, Gordon *151*, 153, 154-5, 156
Franciscis, Professor A. de 40
Franklin, Sir John *95*, 96
Frost, K.T. 23

Gage, Colonel Henry 168
Geldermalsen 7, 190
Geoffrey of Monmouth: King Arthur
   73, *74*, 79
Gildas (monk) 41-2, 44
Giraldus de Barri 76
Glastonbury *73*, *74*-6, 78
Goell, Theresa 63
Golden Hind 125-30; named 126
Gomorrah 16-20
Goneim, Zakaria *48*, 52
Graves and tombs *Title page*, 9, 46-
   101; Absalom *144*, 149-50; Lake
   Guatavita 162
Great Galley 127, 129-30
Greek statues wreck 104-7
Grenville, Sir Richard 120-4
Greyhound 173
Gundry, Thomas Trevenden 177
Gundry-Mills, William 177

Haggerston, Dereck 135
Hartnell, John *95*, 96
Hatcher, Captain Michael 190
Hatton, Sir Christopher 126
Hawkins, Sir John 86-7
Helike 27-9
Henry I: *White Ship* 108-11
Henry II: King Arthur 74-6
Henry VIII: James IV of Scotland 80,
   83; *Mary Rose* 8
Herakleidas of Pontus 28
Herculaneum 37, 38-40
Herihor: tomb *51*, 52
Herod the Great: Hyrcania 148; tomb
   64-8
Herodium *64, 66*, 67-8

Herodotus: Egyptian tombs 53
Hillary, Sir Edmund 97, 101
Hisarlik 138-42, 143
Hitchcock, Edward 20
Hoffman, Dr Charles 113
Holt, J.C. *151*, 155-6
Holzel, Tom 101
Homer: Helike 27; Troy 138-43
Howard, Admiral Sir Thomas 121
Hudson, Henry 92-6
Hwicce people 43
Hyrcania *144*, 148

Ice and snow 96, 97-101
Ika people 162-4
*Illustrated London News: Royal
   Charter* 176
Imhotep: tomb *50*, 51-2
Incas: El Dorado 158-64
Indians of North America: Custer's
   gold 181-5
Irvine, A.S. and family 101
Irvine, Andrew Comyn 'Sandy' 97-101
Isla Verde, Portobelo *86, 89*
Ivett (or Juet), Robert 93-4

Jackson, Professor Kenneth 77
James IV of Scotland 80-5
James Bay, Canada *82*, 93-4
Jebel Fureidis, Herodium 67
Jebel Usdum (Dead Sea) 16-19
Jerusalem: Temple 65-6, 147
Jockey boy statue 106-7
John, King: 'Jewels' 151-7
Jones, John Paul 131-5
Josephus: Essenes 147; Herod the
   Great 65-6; Sodom and Gomorrah
   19-20
Juet (or Ivett), Robert 93-4
Julius Caesar: Alesia 30-5

Karo, Professor George 105-7
Khirbet Mird 148
Khirbet Qumran *144*, 148

La Costa, Juan de 114
Lake Guatavita *159*, 160-2
La Navidád, Hairi 114-5
Lansdown (Mount Badon) *41*, 45
Lebus Palace, Poland 142
Legislation, protective 13, 78, 107,
   150, 162, 173-4, 180, 185
Leland, John 76
Leningrad: Priam's 'treasure' 142
Lepsius, Richard 47
Leucopetra: Vesuvius *36*, 37, 40
Liddington Castle, nr Swindon 42, 44
Little Big Horn (River) 181, 182 , 185;
   Battle 181, *183, 184*
Loch Arkaig *171*, 172-3, *174*
Loch Nam Uamh *171*, 172-3
Longworth, Gil *181*, 182, 184 185
Lot's wife 18-19
Lynch, William Francis 16-17

Macdonalds of Barisdale: loot 173
McKee, Alexander 13
Macleans of Mull: loot 173
McRay, Professor John 68
Mahoney, Derek 78
Mallon, Father Alexis 19
Mallory, George Leigh 97-101
Manetho (Egyptologist) 51
Marigold 125, 126
Marinatos: Atlantis 24-5
Mars 171, 172-3
Marsden, Peter 130
Marsh, Captain *181*, 182-5
Martin, Dr Geoffrey 47
Marx, Robert F. 116-7, *118*

Mary (Drake's ship) 125
Mary Rose 7-8, 9, *12*, 13, 88
Masada 66
'Massacre of the Innocents' 64-5
Maya's tomb 47, 48, 190
Méndez, Diego 116
Menkauhor (Pharaoh) 48
Metal detectors 12-13, *91*
Milik, J.T. 147-50
Milonas, Dr George 106-7
Minoan remains 23-6
Moelfre *175*, 176, 177
Mont Auxois: Alesia 32
Moonshine 121
Morison, Samuel Eliot 116
Mount Everest: Mallory and Irvine 97-
   101
Mount Li, Xi'an *55*, 56-9
Mountain of Nimrod 60-3
Muisca people 160-1, 162, 164
Murlaggan *171*, 173

Nanking cargo 7, 190
Napoleon III: Alesia 32-3
Nazis: Priam's 'treasure' 142-3
Neferkare (Pharaoh) 48
Nemrud Dagh 60-3
Nennius: King Arthur 42-4, 73
Netzer, Professor Ehud *64*, 67-8
Nina 113, 114
Nodjme *51*, 52
Noorbergen, Rene 150
North-West passage: Drake 126;
   Hudson 92-6
Norton, Lt Colonel E.F. 97-101

Odell, Noel 98-100
Oplontis: Vesuvius 37, 39-40
Orde-Powlett, Christopher 170

Parker, William 88-91
Paulet, Sir William 166, *167*
Pausanias: Helike 27-8
Pearson, Captain Richard 132-3
Pelican 125, 126
Perez de Qesada, Herman 160-1
Perrin, Jim 101
Peter Hugh 169
Petrie, Sir W.M. Flinders 51-2
Petrusche Palace, Poland 142
Pharaohs: tombs 47-54; table 49
Philip II of Macedon 54, 189
Piaggi, Father 38
Pi'ankh: tomb 52
Pinta 113
Pizarro, Francisco 158-60
Plato: Atlantis 21-6
Pliny the Elder: Vesuvius 37
Pliny the Younger: Vesuvius 37, 40
Plymouth: *Golden Hind* 125, 127-8
Pockley, John 133-5
Pointe de Barfleur: *White Ship 108*,
   110-11
Pompeii's lost neighbours, 36-40
Porter, General Horace 133
Portobelo, Panama: Drake's coffin 86-
   91, 115
Portsmouth: *Mary Rose 12*
Poseidon/Zeus statue 104-7
Potier, René 35
Prescott, William H. 158-60
Preservation, and protective
   legislation 9-13, 40, 78, 107, 150,
   162, 173-4, 180, 185
Priam's 'treasure' 138-43
Priscus 70-2
Pyramids 48, 51, 52

Qin Shi Huang Di, Emperor 55-9
Quito (Inca city) 160

Qumran 145-6, 148

Radford, Ralegh 78
Raleigh, Sir Walter: El Dorado 161,
  162
Ralph of Coggeshall 152, 157
Renfrew, Professor Colin 8
Rennes-le-Château 9
Resina: Vesuvius 38-9
Revenge 120-4
Reynolds, Eric 177-9
Rijk, Dr Jacobus van 47
Riothamus, (French king) 79
Robot submarines *8*, 9
Roger of Wendover 151, 157
Rogers, Joseph 176
Romer, John 52
Royal Charter: gold 175-80

Sais, Egypt 53
St Ann's Bay, Jamaica 116-8
St John Hope, W.H. *151*, 153, 154, 155
St Michael's Church, Wood Street,
  London *82*, 83-5
San Barnabe 121-2
San Felipe 122
San Salvador 113
Santa María 112-15
Santiago de Palos 115-8
Saqqara, Egypt 47, 48, 51-2
Schliemann, Heinrich and Sophie
  138-43
Schönebeck 142
Schurmacher, Emile C. 185
Scrolls: Dead Sea 144-50; Vesuvius 38
Sea Cadets, Scarborough 135
Secacah *144*, 148
Sekhemkhet (Pharaoh) 48, 51
Seltman, Dr Charles 107
Sepulveda, Antonio de 161
Serapis 132-3
Shi Huang Di 55-9
Shipwrecks 7, 8, 9, *12*, 13, 28, 102-35
Silva, Nunó da 125

Smart, Jack L. *178, 179*, 180
Smith, Professor H.D. 52
Smythe, Sir Thomas 92-3, 94
Sodom and Gomorrah 16-20
Solon: Atlantis 21-3
Sonar equipment 9, 117, *118, 119*
Sora: Vesuvius *36*, 37, 40
Spence, Lewis 23
Stabiae: Vesuvius 37
Stoffel, Colonel 32-3, 35
Stow, John: James IV of Scotland 83
Strabo 27-8
Stuart, Charles Edward: Army payroll
  171-4
Stuart, James Francis 171-2
'Sulis' 44
Summers, William 101
Surrey, Earl of (1513) 80-3
Sutton Bridge *151*, 153, 154
Sutton Grange 154
Swan 125
Swineshead Abbey 151, 152
Syam-Cornu 33-5

Tacitus: Dead Sea 19-20
Tairona people 162-4
Taurania: Vesuvius *36*, 37, 40
Taylor, Captain 176
Terceira, Azores *120*, 122-4
Terracotta warriors 55, 58-9
Terror 173
Terry, General Alfred H. 182, 184, 185
Texas A & M University; Columbus's
  ships 117-8
Thera *22*, 24-6
Therasia *22*, 24
Thompson, Ben 184, 185
Thoresby, Ralph 154
The Times: Golden Hind 129-30;
  Mallory and Irvine 99-100, 101;
  Royal Charter 177
Titanic 7, *8*, 9, 190
Tombs *see* Graves and tombs
Tora *36*, 37, 40

Torre Annunziata 40
Torrington, John 96
Troy *27*, 138-43
Tutankhamun *Title page*, 48-51
Tydd Gote *151*, 155-7

Valley of the Kings 48-54
Vercingétorix 30-5
Vesuvius 37-40
Vila Nova Bay *120*, 122
Vizcaina 91, 115

Wadi Kippa 148
Walpole, Norfolk *151*, 155-7
Walsoken *151*, 154
Walston, Sir Charles 39
Warren, W.L. 156-7
The Wash 151-7
Wellstream 152-3, 154-5, 157
Wen Di, Emperor: tomb 9
Wheaton College Graduate School,
  near Chicago 68
White Ship 108-11
Wignall, Sydney: *Bonhomme Richard*
  133-5; Drake's coffin 89-91; *El
  Gran Grifón* 188; *Revenge* 122-4;
  Royal Charter 177-80; *Santa María
  de la Rosa* 188
William the Atheling 108-11
Wilson, Edward 94-6
Winchester, Marquises of 166, *167*,
  168-70
Wingland 154
Wisbech *151*, 153-5, 156
Wood, John 45
Woods Hole Oceanographic
  Institute: *Titanic* 9
Woolwich: *Golden Hind* 127, 129-30

Xi'an, China 55, 56-9

Zeus/Poseidon statue 104-7

Picture Acknowledgments

Air Photographs Unit, Scottish Development Dept: 174; Alinari, Florence: 65; Alpine Club Library Collection, London: 98, 99, 100; Ashmolean Museum, Oxford: 3 (Griffith Institute), 50; Associated Press Ltd (O. Beattie University of Alberta): 95; BBC Hulton Picture Library: 139, 140, 141A, 188A (Bettmann Archive, N.Y.); Janet and Colin Bord: 75; Werner Braun, Jerusalem: 18, 66, 145; The Bridgeman Art Library: 162; British Library, London: 77, 109R (Cott. Claud Dii Folio 45 verso), 109L (Royal 20A ii Folio 6 verso), 128; British Tourist Authority, London: 43, 127; Christie, Manson & Woods Ltd, Amsterdam: 7; Peter Clayton: 52, 61, 141B; Department of the Environment, London: 169; Harry Margany, Lympne Castle, Kent, in association with The Guildhall, London: 82; Robert Harding Picture Library Ltd, London: 57C, 62A (F. Jackson), 62B (Sassoon); Hirmer Fotoarchiv: 52; *Hull Daily Mail & Times,* Bridlington: 134; Illustrated London News, London: 176; Israel Department of Antiquities: 146; Lincolnshire Library Service: 156; Manchester City Art Gallery: 74; Mansell Collection: 31R, 71, 88, 93 (Tate Gallery), 152, 172, 173, 183, 184; Robert F. Marx: 116, 118, 119; Mary Rose Trust: 158, 161, 163, 164; National Archaeological Museum, Athens/Tap Services: 105, 106; National Galleries of Scotland: 81; National Maritime Museum, Greenwich: 87, 113, 123; National Portrait Gallery, London: 167; Norfolk Archaeological Unit: 155; Osterreichische Nationalbibliothek, Wien: 85; The Peabody Museum of Salem: 133; R. Zev Radovan, Jerusalem: 149; Royal Charter Salvage Expedition Ltd/Ken Jones: 178, 179; Royal Commission on Historical Monuments, England: 84; Scala/Calabri Archaeological Museum: 29; Scari di Pompeii: 39; Sealand Aerial Photography, Chichester: 110; Ronald Sheridan: 24; US Naval Academy Museum, Annapolis: 131; West Air Photography: 45; Sydney Wignall: 89, 90, 124, 134; Ian Wilson: 25, 31L; Woods Hole Oceanographic Institution: 8; Xinhua News Agency: 57B (Zhang Zinmin), 58 (An Kerin).